INDIA ANALYSED

INDIA ANALYSED

Sudhir Kakar

IN CONVERSATION WITH

Ramin Jahanbegloo

OXFORD
UNIVERSITY PRESS

OXFORD
UNIVERSITY PRESS
YMCA Library Building, Jai Singh Road, New Delhi 110001

Oxford University Press is a department of the University of Oxford. It furthers the University's objective of excellence in research, scholarship, and education by publishing worldwide in

Oxford New York
Auckland Cape Town Dar es Salaam Hong Kong Karachi
Kuala Lumpur Madrid Melbourne Mexico City Nairobi
New Delhi Shanghai Taipei Toronto

With offices in
Argentina Austria Brazil Chile Czech Republic France Greece
Guatemala Hungary Italy Japan Poland Portugal Singapore
South Korea Switzerland Thailand Turkey Ukraine Vietnam

Oxford is a registered trade mark of Oxford University Press in the UK and in certain other countries

Published in India by Oxford University Press, New Delhi

First published 2009

ISBN-13: 978-0-19-569893-0
ISBN-10: 0-19-569893-2

Typeset in Perpetua
by Digital Domain, Kolkata
Printed in India at De-Unique, New Delhi 110 018
Published by Oxford University Press
YMCA Library Building, Jai Singh Road, New Delhi 110 001

Contents

Acknowledgements

I would like to express my gratitude to all those who helped me to complete this book. I would like to thank Sudhir Kakar for his kindness, patience, and understanding all through this process. Many thanks also to Katharina Kakar who was a great help in making this book possible. I would also like to thank the Centre for the Study of Developing Societies for their financial and intellectual support. I am also bound to my friends Rajmohan Gandhi, Raj Rewal, Ashis Nandy, and K.C. Singh for their suggestions and insights on the Indian culture. I would be remised if I did not thank my assistant Vinita Priyedarshi for her help in transcribing the conversations. I would also like to thank my mother, Khojasteh Kia, for the encouragement that she has always offered. Last, but not least, I am grateful to my wife, Azin Moalej, who has always given me her love and support when I need it most.

Capturing the Indian Psyche

There are some parts of the world that, no matter how many times you visit, always give you a new sense of reality. For me, India is such a place. Not only because multiple and contradictory views and forms of life co-exist here, but also because this is the home of great souls and strong characters. As Emerson says, 'Character is higher than intellect. A great soul will be strong [enough] to live as well as think.'

Sudhir Kakar is such a man; his peculiar moral strength and integrity of character has had, after seventy years of courageous effort, an ever-growing effect on fellow Indians and other people around the world. I had the privilege of conversing with Kakar and have now developed a deep and abiding friendship with him. He is neither a holy man living on top of a mountain nor a pretentious scholar not willing to listen to and learn from others, but a remarkable human being and a passionate analyst of the Indian cultural imagination, who has studied the explicit link between modernity and tradition in India for more than forty years. Today, Kakar is a well-known name in Indian psychoanalysis and is an influential figure in the international intellectual arena. He has been described by the French magazine *Le Nouvel Observateur* as one of the twenty-five major thinkers of the world. He is the author of novels such as *The Ascetic of Desire*, based on the life of Vatsyayana, and *Ecstasy*, which is an exploration of the relationship between guru and disciple as is seen in the mutual admiration of Miraben and the revered father of the Indian nation, Mahatma Gandhi.

While analysing sexuality as practised in ancient India, Kakar remains a severe critic of the conservative and puritanical sexual mores of contemporary India. As such, his new and fresh translation of the *Kamasutra*, done jointly with Wendy Doniger, appears to be an effort to critique modern Indian sexual behaviours through the presentation of this classical erotic text. The *Kamasutra*, which many tourists who visit India wrongly regard as a textbook about sexual positions, is actually one of the oldest Hindu texts about the art of living. The book provides a fascinating glimpse into the society of ancient India along with much advice on cultivating knowledge of the arts, good manners, and grooming. Kakar's translation and study of the *Kamasutra* recovers and reconstructs the ancient text's insistence on the indispensable balance between the erotic and the spiritual. For Kakar, Indian spirituality is intended to be an intensely practical affair concerned with the alchemy of the libido. Here morality and sexuality are fused together, and it is true that individualism, in its Western form, is foreign to the traditional Indian sexual and spiritual consciousness and experience. For Kakar there are hidden images of individuality incorporated into Indian culture and mystical experiences in India illustrate this fact. But the question which remains at the centre of Kakar's work is: to what extent is psychoanalytic theory that has originated primarily in the Western canon, valid and meaningful when applied to the Indian context? Can the psychological make sense of the cultural in all human experience? The only way to understand Kakar's methodology is to recognize the fact that he has a measure of the modern as well as of the traditional.

Kakar invites his readers to participate in open debates about the universalistic pretensions of psychoanalytic theory when he applies them to Indian culture. A psychological analysis of the Hindu world-image by Kakar makes sense because it provides readers with an analysis of the distinctive features of the Indian social and spiritual structures based on notions such as dharma, moksha, and karma. Realizing that these three coordinates are typical traits of Indian individuality/sociality that are different from Western traits, Kakar contextualizes them in his psychological analysis of India as forms of relational existence.

'The idea that every individual's svadharma is unique,' writes Kakar in his book *The Inner World*, 'enhances a deeply held belief in a pervasive equality at a personal level, among all human beings ... It is more a belief that each individual has a dignified, rightful place and function in the society, a belief which transcends the formal patterns of deference to caste, class, and family hierarchies, but does not hold the promise of an egalitarian society.' In other words, the Hindu mind has a strong inclination to subjectivize timeless mythical events as if they were personal material. 'In India,' affirms Kakar, 'historical events have little immediacy in the lives of individuals; they seem to recede almost instantly into a distant past, to become immemorial legend ... On the other hand, mythical figures like Rama or Hanuman are as actual and as psychologically real (if not more so) as recent historical characters such as Ramakrishna or Shivaji.' This is the reason why, for Kakar, the Oedipus complex is inverted in the Indian context. Kakar chooses the myth of Ganesha to show how the father envies the son for his possessions, including his mother. Kakar's emphasis is also on the goddess as mother and especially as mother of the sons, Ganesha and Skanda, who psychologically represent the two childhood positions of the Indian son. According to Kakar, Skanda and Ganesha personify the two opposing wishes of the older child on the eve of the Oedipus complex: a powerful push for independence and an equally strong pull towards surrender to the maternal from which he has just emerged. Thus in Hindu culture Ganesha's surrender is considered to be superior to Skanda's wish for independence. Therefore, Kakar suggests that unlike the conflicted male of Western thought, the Indian man is at one with the mother's wish to not separate her son from herself.

In his 1986 publication *Tales of Love, Sex and Danger,* co-authored with the New York based psychoanalyst, John Ross, Kakar analyses the 'paradigmatic love story of Hindu India'—the story of the milkmaid Radha and her union with the god Krishna. For Kakar, the Radha–Krishna relation amounts to a 'depersonalized voluptuous state' recalling the earliest attachment of the infant to his mother. What the legendary Radha–Krishna love story illustrates is that in the protected childhood of Indian men there is an absence of social pressure 'to give up non-logical modes of thinking and communication'. An Indian child, thus, in contrast to a Western child, 'is encouraged to continue to live in a mythical, magical world for a long time'. It is interesting to examine Kakar's methodology by understanding the ways in which he presents the Indian cultural viewpoint before applying psychoanalysis to it. Kakar's research on the Indian psyche and sexual behaviours relies profoundly on Indian classical texts, Indian popular culture such as Hindi movies and folktales, and on primary source material such as biographies and letters. Kakar's art lies in the fact that he is a gifted story-teller and a brilliant analyst. Finally, Kakar's contribution to cultural psychology is his technique of interplaying the universalist theoretical approach and the cultural relativist view. As he underlines in his book *Intimate Relations*, 'Indian myths constitute a cultural idiom that aids the individual in the construction and integration of his inner world.'

However, not all Indians agree fully with Kakar's critical analysis of everyday Indian psychological behaviours. Many Indians feel that Kakar's psycho-biographic work on Indian spiritual figures is of a reductionist nature—it fails to appreciate the true essence of Indian mystic traditions correctly. Kakar's response to all these misconceptions and misunderstandings has been: '... mysticism is a kind of individualized religious experience that is limited to very few people; it can be expressed in a society that respects that, and India very much respects mystics. It is comparable to Gandhi: I will not be an ascetic like Gandhi, but I nevertheless respect Gandhi. This means India allows Gandhis to live their lives as it allows mystics to flourish and not put them into any kind of asylum.' What Kakar seems to be reminding us of here is that the ecstatic state of mysticism cannot be achieved without an ascetic state of being. As such, 'Shades of both "infinity" and "personality" will exist in every mystic.' As Kakar shows in his book *The Analyst and the Mystic*, the mystic blends the quest for the divine with the search for a higher self. In this context, the sense of individual identity is used to progress along the spiritual path. As Kakar points out clearly in *The Analyst and the Mystic*, 'Even the passions—lust, anger, greed, inordinate attachment, pride, egoism—which have been traditionally held as obstacles to spiritual progress, do not need to be vanquished in devotional mysticism.' Therefore, for Kakar, the mystical goal is not only to fuse with the Cosmic Being, but also to reach out for a relation with the mother through the 'recovery of a childlike innocence'. Quoting Ramakrishna, Kakar illustrates this relationship of the mystic with the cosmos as one that suggests the child's point of view: 'To my Mother I prayed only for pure devotion … Mother, here is your virtue, here is your vice. Take them both and grant me only pure love for you. Here is your purity and here is your impurity. Take them both Mother and grant me only pure devotion for you. Here is your dharma and here is your adharma. Take them both Mother and grant me only pure devotion for you.' In the course of his analysis of Ramakrishna's private space of passion and desire, Kakar surveys the psychotherapeutic function of the guru as a healer of emotional suffering. The guru is formulated as 'the culturally sanctioned addressee of a collective request for the transforming experience'. Thus in Kakar's formulation, the core of the guru–disciple relationship is 'an increasing surrender to the self–object experience of the merging kind'. In addition to this 'surrender', Kakar says that we can find 'an idealizing transference' in this relationship which touches the deeper layers of the human psyche. What becomes evident here is the expectation of immediate healing by a spiritual teacher rather than a religious promise of gaining a lost paradise. Therefore, while reading Kakar, it becomes clear that for him the two notions of 'spiritual' and 'religious' are not identical.

Looking back at Kakar's life and work, one can easily understand his interest in both religion and spirituality as a form of interplay between the individual and society. According to Kakar, 'It is the core of religion that is important for religious people, and that is spiritual rather than sectarian.' What Kakar calls 'sectarianism' or 'communalism', when viewed psychologically, is a change from the idea of community to that of communalism. Kakar observes that 'religious community is the interactive aspect of religious identity' and what is considered to be dangerous to this identity gives birth to 'communalism and the potential of social violence'. That is to say, religion has a greater emotional intensity and a deeper motivational thrust than ethnic pride or national identity. Taking into account one of Kakar's famous works, *The Colors of Violence*, one should remember that he grew up in a district town in west Punjab where he directly experienced the Partition and the religious confrontation between Hindus and Muslims. It would be wrong, however, to consider Kakar's cultural and psychological writings as the work of a 'Hindu' or a simple analysis of 'Hindu India'. Kakar is more concerned with the spirit of India and what makes the Indianness of Indians rather than with Hindu India. His problem is to understand how one can be an Indian while living with tradition and modernity at the same time. 'I do not look down upon the middle class as betraying the Indian ethos,' observes Kakar, 'because it is creating the ethos for a modern society. The traditional ethos was good for those earlier times. I do not think the Indian identity has emerged yet—this type of contest will go on and on. I think that in society all kinds of changes take place. But there are also parts of it that stay the same.' In other words, what describes the Indian attitude towards life is a certain philosophical relativity and psychological fluidity.

Thus, the Indian *weltanschauung* is one that is beyond the rigid and cynical binary of black and white. Maybe one can say that the Indian ego lives and thinks in that grey zone where there is a permanent exchange between the human soul and the environment. This environment includes the occult and the metaphysical sense of being, and therefore, gurus, shamans, astrologers, and ascetics play an important role in the ongoing reality of the Indian psyche. What makes Indians distinct from the rest of the world is not only the predominance of family, community, and caste in their everyday lives, but also, as Kakar shows in his book *The Indians*, written in collaboration with anthropologist Katharina Kakar, their attitude to sex and marriage, their idea of the 'Other' as we see in the Hindu–Muslim conflict, and their understanding of life and death. However, Kakar is clearly conscious of the complexity and diversity of India when he says, 'How can anyone generalise about a country of a billion people—Hindus, Muslims, Sikhs, Christians, Jains—speaking fourteen major languages and with pronounced differences? How can one postulate anything in common between a people divided not only by social class but also by India's signature system of caste, and with an ethnic diversity characteristic more of past empires than of modern nations?'

And yet, there is an underlying unity in the great diversity of India that needs to be recognized. Interestingly, in India, equality, in the Tocquevillian sense of the term, as a modern social value has not been taken to mean the absence of hierarchy. To quote Sudhir Kakar, 'An Indian has a heightened dependence on external authority figures. An Indian tends to search for authority figures he can idealise, whose "perfection" and omnipotence he can then adopt as his own. Thus, the automatic reverence for superiors is a nearly universal psycho-social fact. And, when it comes to leadership in the larger social institutions of business and government in India, charisma plays an unusually significant role.' As such, old values manifest themselves in the practice of modern values. Indian democracy is strangely adapted to the undemocratic structures of the Indian past. Kakar ascribes the Indian political taste for charisma to 'an unconscious tendency to "submit" to an idealized omnipotent figure, both in the inner world of fantasy and in the outside world of making a living; the lifelong search for someone, a charismatic leader or a guru, who will provide mentorship and a guiding world-view'. The hierarchical nature of the Indian mind applies to all ethnic and caste groups in India. Therefore, democracy in India is not a cultural attitude, but a political value. This is a phenomenon which merits attention.

What makes Kakar's work original is that he presents a composite view of India in which Indians recognize themselves and which helps other people to go beyond their touristic and simplistic view of Indianness. Above all, Kakar remains in dialogue with the key building blocks of Indianness while he interrogates the impact of modernity on Indian society. The works of Sudhir Kakar on the psychosocial tensions underlying Indian identity are a great landmark in understanding the stresses and strains of an unexplored and hidden India which is in the process of aspiring to be authentically traditional and yet is thoroughly modern. Analysing India with Sudhir Kakar, therefore, is not only a way of understanding the Indian way of thinking about the world but also a means to think of the issues in today's world.

RAMIN JAHANBEGLOO
University of Toronto

Part I

From Uttarakhand to Harvard

An Innocent World

RAMIN JAHANBEGLOO (RJ): Let us start these conversations with some preliminary questions about the formative experiences in your childhood that might have pointed you in the direction of your work as an Indian psychoanalyst. You were born in 1938 in Nainital in United Provinces (now Uttarakhand). What are some of your earliest memories of your childhood?

SUDHIR KAKAR (SK): I have no memories of Nainital since I have never been there since I was born. My earliest memories of childhood relate to Punjab where I spent the first fifteen years of my life. My father was in the Provincial Civil Service (PCS) and till I was nine we lived in various towns like Sargodha, Lyallpur, Ludhiana Khurd and, of course, the wonderful city of Lahore, all of which now lie in Pakistan. Both my grandparents lived in Lahore and that is where we went for vacations, family weddings, and festivals. My grandparents from my mother's side were modern, which means that they had adopted such British habits as eating porridge and toast for breakfast, and of men wearing Western clothes when they went out to work in the morning, and of playing tennis or bridge in the evening in

British style clubs. My maternal grandfather was a surgeon who lived in a spacious bungalow in an upmarket area of gardens and well laid-out roads outside the crowded inner city. My father, on the other hand, came from a traditional joint family in the old, inner city. The old part of Lahore was noisy and dirty. Its narrow, winding lanes were lined with overflowing gutters and 2–3 storey houses that leaned against each other so that you could easily cross from the terrace of one house to that of the next. This was the bazaar area where my father's family lived and which teemed with life. His was a close-knit joint family where as a child I could walk into the kitchen that was busy from early morning to late at night and help myself to whatever savouries were being roasted or fried. In the afternoon or at night, drowsy from sleep, I could go into any room and snuggle into bed with an uncle, aunt, or cousin. In contrast, the large rooms of my maternal grandfather's house were mostly empty of people and though well-lit, appeared gloomy to me. There was greater privacy for individuals in that house but also more prohibitions and very little of the indulgence and easy-going acceptance of children that was a feature of my father's traditional family.

RJ: Were your parents religious?

SK: My father who came from a traditional Indian background was an out and out agnostic but my mother, who had a modern upbringing, was quite religious.

RJ: Both your parents were Hindus?

SK: Yes.

RJ: Can you think back about the things you did with your family such as going on trips or vacations? Is there anything that stands out as particularly memorable?

SK: There are many memories that stand out. I can talk about one or two. Once, when I was five years old, my mother was away visiting her parents in Lahore. My father and I were walking along the side of our house in Sargodha when we were attacked by a horde of yellow-tailed wasps and were badly stung. Our faces remained swollen for days. The identification mark entered in my passport as 'Scar over right eye' comes from that painful encounter. Of course, I realized much later that this otherwise banal incident stands out in my memory because it was coupled with a much more fateful one: the birth of my sister. That is why my mother was away. The memory signals the end of a period where I had been the only child of my parents.

Another memory, compressing many others together, is of accompanying my father on his official tours. As a high level administrative functionary, he had to occasionally visit outlying villages of the district to receive complaints and dispense justice. These tours were virtual expeditions with bullock carts and camels loaded with tents, camping equipment, and supplies, setting off early in the morning; while my father and I followed at a more leisurely pace with a retinue of servants, policemen, and court clerks. In the villages, I was fawned over by many people who hoped to curry favour with my father, in the belief that being nice to the son would influence the sire.

RJ: How many brothers and sisters do you have?

SK: I have one younger sister.

RJ: Which kinds of games did you play in your childhood?

SK: Very traditional Indian games like *gulli-danda* and *kabbadi*. I spent hours fishing for non-existent fish in ponds with a thread tied to a twig at one end and a bent pin at the other with a small pellet of dough as the bait.

RJ: Were you an extrovert or an introvert as a child?

SK: I was a shy child except when I was playing games where I was boisterous enough.

RJ: I read somewhere that your grandmother's family had a cinema hall in Lahore, which was lost at the time of Partition and as a child you went there and watched Hindi movies all day long. How old were you at that time and what sort of movies did you watch during those days?

SK: I was 7–8 years old and the movies were costume dramas, with a preponderance of the so-called 'mythologicals', with stirring conflicts between gods and demons. They were quite popular even though we were familiar with every story and how it would end, long before the images began to flicker on the screen.

RJ: Did you like the songs and dances?

SK: Yes, I liked them very much. They were the soul of Indian movies. They still are.

Violence from Afar

RJ: The Partition of India is a subject that one rarely reads about though many books have been written about this period of Indian history. You have also devoted a chapter of your book, *Colors of Violence*, narrating your childhood experiences of the violence that you encountered during Partition. How did you live the Partition of India?

SK: My father was in Rohtak, on the Indian side of Punjab, when the province was partitioned between India and Pakistan in 1947. Members of my father's extended family, and some of their friends who came as refugees from Lahore, took temporary shelter in our home as they sought to begin new lives. As a child, these comings and goings for me were all very exciting. The stories that the refugees told about the dangers they had passed through were thrilling. To me, the Partition was the intrusion of the extraordinary into the ordinary and ordered life of a small child.

RJ: But the experiencc of violence for a child is a terrible thing.

SK: I didn't see the actual violence or only saw it from afar. From the terrace of our house in Civil Lines, I once saw rising pillars of smoke from houses set on fire in the bazaars. My experience of violence was through the stories told by family members whom I had not seen for many years. Yes, they had suffered terribly. Some wept while narrating their woes. But what I registered, and shared, was the exaltation of a tribe that had come unscathed through enemy territory rather than the violence it had gone through.

RJ: In your book, *Colors of Violence*, you say that you became aware of how your extended family's 'war stories' had become the core of your memory of the Muslim in general. May I ask you how you perceived the Muslims in your adolescence before your psycho-historical account of violence between Hindus and Muslims during the Partition?

SK: I have two sorts of memories of Muslims. One is of early childhood when we lived in Sargodha and Lyallpur, and where most of our servants were Muslims. They spoilt me completely and their children were my best friends. My first love was the twelve-year old Fatima, the daughter of the Pathan office peon; I was four or five. The other set of memories are from the Partition time when Muslims were presented as the 'Enemy', as rapists and killers, each one of them! The stand-out image of these latter memories is of an archetypal Muslim butcher in his *lungi* and blood-flecked undershirt running down the street, waving his big knife which would stab any Hindu who came in his way. Both these perceptions co-existed and perhaps continue to do so in the subconscious part of my mind.

RJ: India is a country of diversity of religions. How did you live this phenomenon in your childhood?

SK: As part of a very natural order. I remember that my father's boss in Sargodha was a Muslim, and then there were his Sikh and Hindu colleagues. The differences were never thought of in terms of religious affiliation but in certain ways of life, mostly related to eating habits. My grandmother would never invite a Muslim to eat with us. One did become aware of the difference in the celebration of religious festivals but that was not felt as threatening but rather an occasion of wonderment and new source of entertainment.

RJ: The eating parts that you talk about remind me of Tagore's family. Is that a serious thing in Hindu culture?

SK: Yes. For Muslims, eating from the same plates implies brotherhood but among the Hindus, it involves the notions of pollution. The idea of your food being touched by fingers that have been in another mouth is felt to be deeply polluting and evokes visceral disgust.

RJ: It means that in India you can share the public but not the private?

SK: Yes, and this division has stayed in India for a very long time. As a child, I ate with non-Hindus but after I was 4–5 years old, I was forbidden to eat with them.

RJ: But how does that happen? Does it become a taboo?

SK: No, it is not a taboo. The adults don't call you a dirty boy if you eat with Muslims but the ill-concealed aversion on their faces if you have done so conveys an unmistakable message.

RJ: So that means that as a child you are not aware of the taboos but as you grow older, you realize it. That is very interesting. Some Indians who suffered directly due to the Partition talk about it in terms of a Holocaust. Do you think of the Partition as a traumatic rupture in the Indian psyche?

SK: I think so. It touches the North Indian, especially the Punjabi psyche, and also the Bengali psyche more than those in South India who did not have a first-hand experience of the horrific violence.

RJ: Is it still very difficult for the Indians, especially those of the state of Punjab, to talk about Partition?

SK: The first-hand memories are those of the older generation, which has begun to die out. For them, it is no longer that difficult to talk of events which are now more than six decades old. But the succeeding generation's memories are second-hand, without elaboration or narrative quality. They are less of memories and more of feelings and attitudes towards the Muslims absorbed in early childhood from their parents or grandparents.

The Partition Trauma

RJ: Would you say that the Partition trauma is still an unsolved enigma in the Indian psyche?

SK: It is like a bone sticking in your throat, which you can neither throw out nor swallow.

RJ: In which way do you think it could be swallowed once and for all?

SK: Certainly not by revisiting the Partition in a dry factual way, at an academic level. We need to involve imagination as much as reason, if not more so, to change mindsets. Our history books or other educational material do not do that. We need to take the assistance of literature, cinema, and art to make our stories about the Partition emotionally compelling. But after sixty years, all we have is just a couple of novels and a handful of stories written about that traumatic moment in our history.

RJ: Before Partition, what was the perception of the British in your family?

SK: There were two kinds of perceptions. My paternal grandfather, who was a contractor, was a big supporter of the Congress Party. He built some of the main British government buildings in Lahore. Because of his increasing sympathy for the Congress Party and involvement in the freedom struggle, he stopped taking contracts from the British government. He was very close to the Punjabi leader Lala Lajpat Rai. He was a gentleman and I never heard him abuse the British. There was no anger in him against them though he wished them out of the country. My father, who was a Civil Servant, admired the British. He genuinely thought that they had brought modern civilization to India. He thought that the British were honest while the Indians were venal and dishonest. I think I grew up with ambivalence towards the British, imbibing some of my father's attitudes while disliking his obsequiousness towards his British superiors. Unlike many of my generation, I never felt particularly attracted by Britain, nor did I want to go and study at a British university.

RJ: Did you grow up with a British education in the family?

SK: I did but not my father.

RJ: I mean in the family and not at school. Did your father introduce you to British literature and culture?

SK: As I said, my father was divided in himself because he had strong Indian roots, and was fluent in Sanskrit and Urdu, but had joined the Civil Service. He was very good with written English but made mistakes while speaking it since he knew many words only from his reading. I remember that my mother who was Convent-educated would laugh at him when he mispronounced an English word. I am ashamed to say that we, the children, joined in the laughter, though my father took it very well. In fact, our laughter was an affirmation of the success of his project in having a modern, Westernized family. He had a large collection of English books, including the classics, and they were naturally available to me without his formally introducing me to English literature.

RJ: Did you read novels by Charles Dickens or Jane Austen?

SK: As a boy, I read the typical literature of an English schoolboy—the Williams series, the Biggles series, the detective stories of Agatha Christie, Dorothy Sayers, and Sherlock Holmes as also such books as *Treasure Island*, *Ivanhoe*, *Robinson Crusoe*, *Gulliver's Travels*, and so on. By the age of 14, I had read quite a lot of British stuff.

Imagining Gandhi

RJ: What image did you have of Gandhi in those days? Did you consider him a hero?

SK: I have considered Gandhi as a hero for a very long time. I remember that during my school vacations, I had once gone to stay at my grant-aunt's house in Delhi. One evening, she took me along to attend one of Gandhi's prayer meetings. As Gandhi made his way through the crowd, he passed very near us. My grant-aunt told me to touch his feet, which I did. I felt very proud. But during the Partition, when my family members came as refugees, I realized that they looked down upon Gandhi as a weak man, who was responsible for the tragedy that had befallen them. He was a 'Muslim lover' to them. My grandmother hated him. Whenever Gandhi came on the radio, she would cruelly mimic his speech, hissing out every 's' as 'sh', the way Gandhi spoke the consonant because of his missing front teeth. My father admired Gandhi but as a magistrate, he would probably have put him behind bars if he had ever appeared in his court, charging him with sedition against the British Raj.

RJ: I think that India has both a saintly image of Gandhi and a political historical view. In what way did you have a saintly or a political view of Gandhi?

SK: During the Partition, my image of Gandhi became more political. The saintly image existed before 1947 and then reappeared much later in adulthood.

RJ: How would you relate to the need for a saint in Indian culture?

SK: I think this is an old and persisting need. Partly, the need is cultural. It has to do with the high value placed on spiritual life and the saint being considered the earthly representative of the 'spirit'. Partly, the need goes back to the structure of the Indian family wherein a singular paternal voice is diffused among many voices of other adults of the extended family. Thus, there is an unfulfilled need in the child for the guiding voice of an ideal, ever-present father, which is then embodied by the saint–guru.

RJ: Is that why they called Gandhi 'Bapu'?

SK: Yes.

RJ: Do you think that India still relates to the figure of Gandhi?

SK: The relationship with Gandhi keeps changing, from a modernist dismissal of him as a faddish crank to his idealization as the prophet and visionary of a desirable world, and back again. The fascination with him, though, endures. That has not disappeared. In fact, at present, Gandhi again looms large in our collective consciousness. Personally, as an unregenerate romantic, my view of Gandhi tends towards idealization. In my new book *Mad and Divine: Spirit and Psyche in the Modern World*, I have a chapter on Gandhi as a pioneer in the art of practical spirituality, that is, a spirituality which is not contemplative or ecstatic but is rather tantamount to being a spiritual way of living in and engaging with the world. When you go through Gandhi's life and writings, then you observe that it is his practical spirituality which runs as a common theme through all his actions and strivings. For example, he never considered non-violence as just a tactic in a struggle against oppression. To him, non-violence was significant only if there was a vision of love behind it. Without that vision of love, such actions, or in fact any altruistic action, does not possess any special merit.

RJ: When I look at the international framework, I have the feeling that Gandhi is more important on a political basis; and his non-violence as a political strategy, which was practised by Nelson Mandela in South Africa or by Lech Walesa in Poland, is becoming more important than his saintly image. But I think that Gandhi and Gandhism in India are more symbolic of a moral view at the back of the Indian sub-consciousness, and today we talk more about 'Gandhigirism' against 'Dadagirism' as put into image by Bollywood (Hindi cinema).

SK: The interesting thing is that non-violence had different aspects for Gandhi. As I said just now, if non-violence is not backed by a vision of love in the non-violent register, then any kind of 'Gandhigiri' or 'Gandhism' is only half of Gandhi, and not even the half he considered as his essence.

Encounters with Spirituality

RJ: After the Partition, your life changed and it was narrowed down by the world of Christian missionary schools.

SK: There wasn't much Christianity going around in the missionary school. There was a coloured lithograph of Jesus with a bleeding heart hanging on some walls of the school building but that was about the extent of the missionary message.

RJ: Do you have memories of your professors and your schoolmates?

SK: Oh yes, many, though I have lost touch with all my school friends. I remember a good-looking Kashmiri boy who had joined my class and who played some innocent prank. The teacher, a Brother Conway, started beating him and could not stop even after the boy had dirtied his pants. This was hidden sadism that was coming out in these celibate and otherwise such dedicated missionary teachers. There was a good deal of repression, sexual and otherwise, that was going on in such places. I remember this incident as I sensed that what had happened signified more than punishment for an offense, that there were other hidden forces behind it.

RJ: You talked about the portrait of Jesus on the school wall. Did you talk about religion in the school?

SK: No, religion didn't matter. To me, religion was associated with festivals like Diwali and Dusshera. I remember that I sometimes went to a temple with my mother for a festival but that was rare. My religious education was an experiential one, associated with festival celebrations, and was related to the excitement of eating special foods, wearing new clothes, and meeting relatives. It had nothing to do with instruction in religious beliefs and ideas.

RJ: Would you distinguish between religion and spirituality?

SK: To me, religious ideas and beliefs are totally unimportant. What is important is the religious experience which I would call spirituality and that has nothing to do with religious ideas about God, the after-life or morality.

RJ: This reminds me of what Maulana Azad said about religion. He said: 'Religion teaches us that life is a duty which must be fulfilled. It is a burden which must be borne.' Do you accept this view?

SK: Yes.

RJ: You do consider yourself a spiritual person?

SK: Yes, spiritual in the sense that the agnostic part of my father and the religious part of my mother have continued to co-exist in me, making me unfit for any traditional faith or belief system. If oneness with the Divine, the *unio mystica*, is the summit of spirituality and the base camp is what the Buddhists call compassion, then I would be content to reach the starting point of the spiritual expedition, which is tolerance. I hope I can reach the starting point and do not even aspire to the summit.

RJ: Which subjects did you like in school?

SK: I liked Chemistry, History, and Maths. I liked Chemistry because of the smell of the laboratory.

RJ: Did you like literature?

SK: I loved it, though not the way it was taught at school.

RJ: You read novels?

SK: Yes. I started with Hindi novels when I was very young, influenced by my father's youngest sister who devoured these romances and passed them along, irrespective of whether they were or were not suitable for a young child's sensibilities. In adolescence, I discovered English literature but my interest expanded rapidly to include translations of French and Russian novels. I remember that my father had the English translation of Balzac's *Droll Stories* hidden behind a stack of other books because it was, regarded as sexually explicit and unsuitable for a growing boy. It was, of course, the first book that I read when I rummaged through his books in his absence.

RJ: But it was much later that you got the taste of writing?

SK: Yes. In my early twenties.

An Idea of Germany

RJ: Did you have an idea that you would be a writer?

SK: No, I wanted to be like my father, a civil servant.

RJ: Why did you choose engineering after your college?

SK: There were three options for me: engineering, medicine, and civil services. I invariably fainted at the site of blood, so medicine would have been a bad choice. After two years of college in Jaipur, I wrote a university exam in which I secured a first division but only got the sixth rank. Since I did not stand first, as I had done since the beginning of my school years and as my father routinely expected, he thought that I would not pass the Indian Administrative Examination (IAS) and so should study engineering instead, which would at least secure me a safe livelihood. For middle class children and their parents, financial security was the prime consideration in the selection of a career. So I went to study mechanical engineering in Ahmedabad.

RJ: Did you like it?

SK: No, I hated it. Maths was fine but I disliked carpentry and all the mechanical stuff.

RJ: Is that why you turned to economics?

SK: No, not because of that. I finished my engineering and then went to Calcutta for one year to work there as an apprentice in a sewing machine factory. Germany was one of the three countries that was considered good for further education in engineering. United States was too expensive and I did not want to go to the UK, so I landed up in a shipyard in Hamburg. Hamburg was very far away from India. There were no long distance phone calls in those days or at least impoverished Indians like myself were not expected to make them. Letters to and from India took weeks. The situation was ideal for me to rebel. So I rebelled and wrote to my father that I did not want to be an engineer anymore. I wanted to study Philosophy instead. At the time, I believed that the future of philosophy lay in Theoretical Physics. My intention was to study Physics at the University of Goettingen. My father rightly thought that all this was nonsense as I would never earn money by being a philosopher. He was vigorously supported by my mother's father, the surgeon, who was duly consulted, and who advised my father to nip such fanciful ideas in the bud, that there were enough woolly headed people roaming around in our country. The correspondence with my father went to and fro, but luckily I was far away and at a safe distance from family pressures. We finally reached a compromise that I could study Economics, which was seen as a compromise between engineering and physics, a 'soft' discipline as compared to engineering but at least one in which I would not starve.

RJ: But you started to learn German only because of engineering?

SK: Yes, though I never learnt it formally.

RJ: How did you perceive Germany and German culture in those years?

SK: There were very few coloured foreigners in Germany at the time. I am talking of the beginning of the 1960s. I was thus an exotic breed, more desired than disdained. I was like a puppy dog, wagging his tail and being petted by most people who were not allergic to dogs. Still, renting a room to live in was never easy. I wasn't aware of racism and believed the excuses various landladies offered me at the time for their inability to rent me the room. Looking back, my situation seems to be represented by the orientalist paintings of Eugène Delacroix: an African boy with wide open eyes and curly hair standing in the middle of richly dressed white aristocrats lounging around in various states of ease.

RJ: So they had no idea of where India was or what it looked like?

SK: Most of them had no idea. They had seen some images of India through movies. I remember that one of the movies showing at that time was Fritz Lang's *The Tiger of Eschnapur*. From the title, you can imagine what the movie was like. So they had an image of India but it was an image that was both exotic and racist.

RJ: You had to learn German?

SK: I didn't have to do it. I was a very good table tennis player and, in fact, was the Gujarat champion for many years. Whenever I went to a new city, I immediately made for a table tennis club. This is what I did in Hamburg too—where the club took care of me since they wanted me to play for their team. I immediately made friends and never felt lonely. I didn't learn German officially but picked it up in the shipyard and in interactions with people. In the beginning, it consisted of a lot of the slang of the dockyards.

RJ: You said that you were not political.

SK: Yes. I was quite apolitical but I was in radical company in the city of Mannheim where I went to the university. My friends were leftist intellectuals and anarchist painters, and I thoroughly enjoyed night-long discussions about politics, art, literature, and cinema, over innumerable mugs of beer. Together with them, I marched in the annual anti-atomic weapons demonstration though I must confess that my participation was less political than dictated by the hope of getting close to a girl who believed in the cause. Luckily, German universities were very relaxed in those days. You didn't have to attend classes as long as you passed your exams.

RJ: What led you to read Sigmund Freud?

SK: When I was in engineering college, I read *Interpretation of Dreams*, which impressed me very much. But I never thought of becoming a psychoanalyst at that time. I remember that when I went to Calcutta to work, I had a pretty cousin whom I tried to impress by analysing her dreams.

RJ: How did you perceive the German culture in those days? Was it just through your reading or also through experiencing it?

SK: The German culture in those days was the culture of my friends—writers and artists. My best friend was a painter who had been an assistant of Oskar Kokoschka. I had no idea of Western classical music at the time, which to me seemed pretty discordant. One of my friends took me to a Mozart concert which I enjoyed, and thereafter I started appreciating Western classical music. Another friend introduced me to jazz, the 'cool' jazz of the time: Miles Davis, Gerry Mulligan, and the like. I became very fond of jazz. In fact, when I came back to India, I learnt playing the *tabla* for a couple of years in the hope of playing the Indian drums in a jazz band. But my sense of rhythm was much less than the height of my aspiration. I was also introduced to contemporary German literature by my friends: Heinrich Böll, Günter Grass, Martin Walser, and so on.

RJ: Did you read any German philosophers?

SK: Psychology yes, but philosophy no. My German was not good enough to understand the difficult prose of philosophers like Heidegger, Husserl, or Hegel.

RJ: Did you have any interests regarding radicalism or hippism?

SK: No, this interest started in America in the mid-1960s. In Germany of the early 1960s, when I was there, the so-called counter culture had not yet made an appearance though Rock-n-Roll was becoming quite a hit.

RJ: Did you like Rock-n-Roll?

SK: I liked dancing to its music and still do. I even tried to take dance lessons in Germany but soon gave up.

RJ: I went to France in an early age like you and I remember that I found myself in a completely different surrounding, with new people, and new ways of living and eating. Did all that come to you naturally?

SK: Yes, absolutely. I think it came from the early preparation which my father gave me since he thought all prohibitions with regard to eating were irrational. We had no taboos on what to eat or what not to eat. I ate anything I liked.

RJ: So you already had it in your family?

SK: No, not in the extended family or with my mother. But I knew that that there were very few taboos with regard to food in my father's mind.

RJ: You always maintained contact with your family and your parents.

SK: Yes, it was a strong emotional bond. I always wanted them to come to Europe so that I could show them around, but it never happened.

RJ: Maybe you have a different perception now in your older age when your parents are not there, but did you perceive them as an invisible moral authority that was always there?

SK: No, not as a moral authority but as gentle guides. Morally they would have disapproved of some of my youthful sowing of wild oats in Germany. But I was always assured of their unquestioning support. They were like the safe harbour from where I could venture out and explore the world's cultures.

RJ: I asked you this question because I read in Gandhi's biography that when he was going abroad, he had to make several vows to his mother and the invisible authority was always there in his mind while he was studying in England.

SK: No, I didn't have that kind of moral authority in my mind. I thought of my parents as encouraging and applauding my ventures rather than as prohibiting them.

The Beautiful Mind of Erik Erikson

RJ: Why did you decide to come back to India?

SK: Because of my family which I loved very much. They were India for me; though subliminally I also missed the sights, sounds, and smells of the country. When I came back to India the first time in 1964, after an absence of five years, I was very unhappy. It was very difficult for me, especially since I did not know what to do with my life.

RJ: But you went to Ahmedabad and started teaching management at the Indian Institute of Management (IIM) there.

SK: No, I started as a Research Fellow at the IIM, Ahmedabad, for lack of anything else to do.

RJ: Why did you choose Gujarat?

SK: Because my aunt, with whom I had stayed when I studied engineering and who I was very close to, lived in Ahmedabad.

RJ: This is where you met Erik Erikson and your life changed.

SK: Thank God.

RJ: Was it an immediate impact?

SK: No, the impact came three months after we had been together. But I was so ready for it. I was going through an intense emotional crisis. One day, I would want to go to Poland to study to become a film director and the next day I wanted to become a philosopher. At that time, it was difficult to go to Eastern Europe which was behind the Iron Curtain. The only way to study in a Soviet-bloc country was through an educational exchange programme with that particular country, which was administered by the Government of India. I had a distant relative who was a high official in the Ministry of Education, and I thought I had a good chance to go to Poland. But he informed my parents that I had gone crazy as I had applied to join the National Film School in Lodz. Had my application not gone through this distant relative I would perhaps have been a film director. I would have loved making highly psychological movies like Ingmar Bergman, whom I idolized at the time.

RJ: You were experimenting with life in those days?

SK: I was experimenting with life and the various roles I could play in its puppet theatre. In Germany, I had started writing short stories about India and even had a fellowship for young writers to spend three months in the south of France. I did not earn much through writing but enough to buy things like a winter jacket or afford a good meal once in a while.

RJ: Let's go back to your encounter with Erik Erikson. What sort of a person was he?

SK: He was a wonderful and gentle man, with a wary sense of humour. He always gave his full attention to whichever person he was with at any particular time. He also had what I would call a generosity of the spirit. Even if he was teaching a seminar where I thought some students were talking nonsense, he would listen carefully to what was being said. He would then repeat what the person had said but add something of his own to it, and thus transform the person's contribution into something interesting and insightful. You could see the delight on the student's face, with an expression of 'Did I say this?' flitting across his features. Many professors have the habit of cutting a student down. Erikson was never like that and this is one of the many lessons I learnt from him. He was very tolerant and generous with his time for me. After all, to him I must have been just a confused young Indian, who had studied engineering and economics, and now had the crazy idea that he wanted to be a filmmaker. I used to pour out my heart to him.

RJ: It was a kind of therapy.

SK: Absolutely. I was going through an identity crisis and was lucky to meet the person who had discovered the syndrome and gave it that name.

RJ: How did you encounter him?

SK: My aunt had a house, which also had a small guesthouse attached to it, where I lived. She had gone to the USA and had rented out her own place to Erikson and his wife. He had come to Ahmedabad for a few months to undertake research for his book on Gandhi. I helped Erikson with little things like telling him where he could get a particular book, or filling up on the background of a particular person he was going to meet, or translating some of the stuff available only in Hindi.

RJ: So you helped him before being his assistant?

SK: Yes.

RJ: Did you go with him to the Sabarmati Ashram?

SK: No.

RJ: Did he talk to you about his views on India or about his theories on psychohistory?

SK: We talked about India but I had no idea of what psychohistory was.

RJ: What were his views on India in those days before he wrote the book on Gandhi?

SK: He was very positive about India. He had grown up in an era before World War I, in which many European artists and intellectuals had a romantic idealization of India.

RJ: Was he an academic or a scientific person?

SK: He was more intuitive than a systematizer. He was impressionistic and insightful, more adept at seeing patterns in a picture rather than at building arguments. That is something I identify with. As one gets older, one does miss out on the details but sees the pattern more clearly.

RJ: What sort of questions did you ask him?

SK: Unfortunately, too few. My main interest was that he should listen to me. I talked a lot about myself.

RJ: Did he understand that you were interested in psychoanalysis?

SK: No, he did not. Neither did he direct me to it. My interest in psychoanalysis came not through the head but through the heart. It was not an intellectual interest but more of a conversion experience. I wanted to be like him, become the kind of person he was and if that included being a psychoanalyst, then so be it. I did read his two books: *Young Man Luther* and *Childhood and Society* at that time.

RJ: Did you also talk about Gandhi? What were his views on Gandhi?

SK: He was very positive about Gandhi until he got stuck in the middle of his writing because of what he considered as Gandhi's cruelty toward two teenagers in his South African ashram, who had evinced sexual interest in each other. Erikson was quite upset and could not write for many days. A callow youth, I was blithely negative about Gandhi because of what I considered his silly sexual ideas and even sillier food taboos. Erikson made me appreciate Gandhi much more than it would have been otherwise.

RJ: What interested him in Gandhi, non-violence or saintlyhood?

SK: I think it was the spirituality of non-violence. Erikson was quite a spiritually inclined person himself.

RJ: Was he a religious man?

SK: I think he was. I did not talk to him about religion. Psychoanalysis was very anti-religious at that time. It still is, though the hostility has somewhat diminished of late. Erikson could not be a card-carrying psychoanalyst and openly religious at the same time.

RJ: In the early 1960s, he had a very idealistic view of Gandhi which changed later.

SK: True. His book talks very positively and admiringly about Gandhi.

RJ: What interested me in his book, *Gandhi's Truth*, is his methodology, the way he put together the meaning of historical events with an individual's developmental history, something which you don't find in any other psychoanalyst's work.

SK: Yes, the meaning of an event only derives from a configuration, what I call Erikson's 'fourfold path'.

RJ: Can we talk more about it? I think that was the core of Erikson's theory?

SK: Yes, especially since it has also influenced my own work. Briefly, the meaning of an event in an individual's life needs to be looked at in four different contexts. First, what does the event mean at the individual's stage of life when it happens? Second, what meaning does the event have in the individual's life history? Third, what does the event mean in the context of his group and fourth, what is the meaning of the event in the history of the group? You can get the true meaning of an event only if you explore it in all the four contexts rather than when you limit yourself to only one context. The method thus elegantly combines psychology, sociology, and history.

Between Gandhi and Freud

RJ: Was he in favour of a dialogue between the East and the West?

SK: Not in that sense. He was very much in favour of a dialogue between Freud and Gandhi, which he incorporates at the end of his book. I feel that he wanted to bring psychoanalysis and spirituality together, not East and West.

RJ: Did he see how his ideas fitted into Hindu ideas?

SK: Yes. In fact, that was the subject of the first paper I ever published, a comparison of the Eriksonian stages of life and the Hindu scheme of ashramdharma. It appeared in *Philosophy East and West*.

RJ: Obviously, Erikson saw in the principle of dharma a convenient way of seeing man's continuous efforts and struggle.

SK: Yes, he was interested in knowing more about the various concepts of dharma. In Ahmedabad, he discussed these ideas at a couple of seminars.

RJ: Would you say that *Gandhi's Truth* is a book about a charismatic personality or about non-violence as a form of therapy? Was Erikson interested in non-violence as a form of therapy?

SK: He saw non-violence as a therapy for the world's problems just as psychoanalysis is a non-violent way of engaging with an individual's conflicts. I think this was also because the Vietnam War was going on in those days and there was a lot of unease and unrest about violence in the world.

RJ: He was also interested in Gandhi as a charismatic personality?

SK: Yes, as a positive charismatic personality, though he also wrote about Hitler and the evils of charisma.

RJ: I think that for Erikson, Gandhi was above all a kind of man who could sense a universal danger and find a solution for it.

SK: Yes.

RJ: After you met Erikson and discussed your identity crisis with him, he suggested that you should earn a PhD and then join him at Harvard. How did that work out?

SK: When I told him that I wanted to be like him, he told me that I would have to finish my doctorate as fast as I could and then he would call me to Harvard as his assistant. So I went to Vienna for my doctorate and then on to Harvard to become his assistant and a Lecturer in General Education at the University. He kept his promise.

RJ: So your true encounter with psychoanalysis began only at Harvard?

SK: Yes, I learnt psychoanalysis by teaching it. I had to teach in his course, which was called 'The Human Lifecycle'. After his class, I was supposed to discuss the readings for the day with a section of the students. I had to study the prescribed readings and keep at least one day ahead of my students. That was the beginning of my psychoanalytic education.

RJ: Was it related to his eight stages of man's life?

SK: Yes, the course was built around these stages.

RJ: How were the surroundings at Harvard, intellectually and academically?

SK: They were very interesting. This was the time of the Vietnam War, 'flower power', 'Make love, not war', and, of course, the Beatles. I was a snob though and did not think that the Beatles were that great. I was more interested in cool jazz and Western classical music. The students who took the course were very serious and very bright. I became friendly with many of the students, especially those in the Harvard theatre group. But there was also a lot of affectation at Harvard. Many students and teachers of moderate accomplishment, even visiting scholars, believed they that were something special just because they were a part of Harvard. That kind of borrowed glory still exists among some who have been at Harvard.

RJ: Was Erikson famous at that time?

SK: Very famous. George Bundy was the Dean of Faculty at Harvard at that time. He had brought Erikson to Harvard as a University Professor even though Erikson had only a high school diploma, not even a BA degree. His classes were always full and he was a guru for many students.

RJ: Maybe also because he was socially active and radical in his thoughts?

SK: Perhaps, though his activism was a quiet affair, of the mind.

PART II

The Making of an Indian Analyst

Common Shared Values

RJ: Were you interested in other psychoanalytical movements like the Freudian Marxism of Herbert Marcuse and Erich Fromm?

SK: At that time, three psychoanalysts were prominent in the counterculture movement and were widely read: Herbert Marcuse, RD Laing, and Erich Fromm.

RJ: Did you ever meet any one of these three?

SK: No.

RJ: Did you go to any Congresses of psychoanalysis?

SK: No, I was not really a psychoanalyst, just a learner. For one year, I was also a Research Fellow at the Harvard Business School, where there was a professor who wanted to incorporate psychoanalytic ideas into Management. At the Harvard Business School, I worked in the Programme on Social Psychology of Management and wrote my first book, a psychobiography of Frederick Taylor, the 'Father of Scientific Management', which was published by MIT Press. Psychoanalysis in the sense of becoming an analyst came much later. I wanted to be a psychoanalyst but couldn't be one in America as at that time only those with a medical degree were admitted to the training programmes of the psychoanalytic institutes. Only a few very eminent people like the Harvard sociologist Talcott Parsons and the psychologist Robert White were allowed to undergo psychoanalytic training but were not permitted to practise as analysts. I returned to India.

RJ: In which year?

SK: In 1968. I came back to IIM, Ahmedabad, as an Assistant Professor and then became a Professor in Organizational Behaviour. I stayed at IIM for three years but since my heart was set on being a psychoanalyst, I resigned and went abroad for my training. Since this was not possible in USA, Erikson wrote to a well-known German analyst, Alexander Mitscherlich, the director of the Psychoanalytic Institute in Frankfurt, who made it possible. Mitscherlich also got me a day-job as a researcher in a market research firm so that I could pay for my psychoanalytic training, which included five hours a week of personal analysis that every aspiring psychoanalyst must go through.

RJ: How many years did you spend there?

SK: Four years. I then went to Vienna for a year as a visiting professor and then came back to Delhi to set up my practice. The only problem was that in India, hardly any one knew about psychoanalysis at that time and so it was difficult to start a practice. The Indian Council of Social Science Research (ICSSR) had given me a fellowship and I had some money for the first year till I got some patients.

RJ: Were there any Indian psychoanalysts who were Freudian before you?

SK: Oh yes. The Indian Psychoanalytic Society is very old. It goes back to 1929. There were psychoanalysts in Calcutta and there were some based in Bombay.

RJ: You did not go to see them?

SK: No.

RJ: Did they have to approve your practice?

SK: Yes. I became a member of the Indian Psychoanalytic Society and went to Calcutta once to present my membership paper on the treatment of two cases.

RJ: Erikson always used to say that clinical work is research in progress. Maybe that is why he was attempting a kind of long-range contemplation beyond the only horizons of Western culture. Was he interested in other cultures than Indian?

SK: Erikson had a great interest in anthropology and was a part of two anthropological expeditions. One was to the Sioux tribe of American Indians with Scudder Mekeel, and the other was to another Indian tribe, the Yurok, with Alfred Kroeber. He had long discussions with Margaret Mead and Gregory Bateson. Mead was a great friend of his.

RJ: In your article, 'The Traditional Hindu Views and Psychology of Erikson', you make a comparison between Erikson's eight stages of life and the Hindu theory of the stages of life. Was Erikson attentive to the points of convergence and divergence between common Hindu therapy and his own therapy?

SK: Yes, he was, since this was the time when he was writing *Gandhi's Truth,* on the origins of militant non-violence. He read my paper carefully and jotted down notes and suggestions in the margin.

RJ: Where were the comparisons between his theory and the dharma theory?

SK: Erikson has said, different stages of life have different tasks and different normative crises, as also unique strengths that may emerge from a specific crisis. The tasks and the possible strengths of his stages of life are very similar to the Hindu stages of ashram dharma. He found the convergence striking; though the Hindu theory does not take the first three stages of Erikson's model into account and emphasizes the social part of Erikson's psychosexual stages more than their psychological aspects.

RJ: But he was a relativist?

SK: Very much so.

RJ: So he did not really agree with a universal theory of man?

SK: No, the fact that he was a relativist means that he did not believe that there is only one theory of Man but a spectrum on which different theories lie. The spectrum, of course, has limits and thus he was not a post-modernist in the sense of 'Anything goes!' For instance, in answer to how much nurture one should give a growing child, he believed that between a minimum of events that must happen to keep a baby psychologically alive, and a maximum frustration beyond which its development would be permanently stunted, there is a leeway, and that different cultures decide what they consider workable and insist on calling necessary.

RJ: Do you consider yourself to be a relativist?

SK: Yes, in the sense of what I have just said. Not a complete relativist but a believer in relativity within wide limits imposed by the universal aspects of human nature. This universality, though, is much broader in scope than has been defined by any single culture, including cultures of social science.

RJ: Do you believe that there are common shared values in human beings?

SK: Yes, I believe there are. And if they are not, then maybe we need to define universal not as what human beings share in common but what they *should* have in common.

RJ: So it's not ontological, but de-ontological, like human rights?

SK: Yes.

Reading Freud in India

RJ: How did you find the balance between Western psychoanalysis and Hindu myths? Was it difficult for you to find this balance because psychoanalysis per se is based on modern rationality?

SK: In the beginning it was difficult because when one starts out as an analyst, one is, of course, more orthodox than the Pope. But if one is open to experience, one's practice starts rubbing-in the message that the human psyche may not completely fit in with psychoanalytic models, and that there may be cultural variations. I was lucky in this since there was no psychoanalytic institute in Delhi, I could develop my ideas without fear of deviation from orthodoxy, which would attract censure from other colleagues. What used to happen in most psychoanalytic institutes in the West at the time was that any deviation from the Freudian canon was severely combated, which meant that people did not take chances. I was lucky in one respect that I had no colleagues. But the negative part of having no colleagues is that your speculations are not checked. My psychoanalysis was already influenced by Erikson's relativistic stance, so it was not kosher Freudian in any case. I think that Erikson called himself Freudian all the time because he did not want to be thrown out of the psychoanalytic movement, which was his only home. He didn't believe in the entire Freudian theory but kept his disagreements quiet or muted them. Not that I reject Freud. Not at all. I completely subscribe to his basic assumptions, such as the importance of the unconscious part of the mind in our thought, behaviour, and action, the vital significance of early childhood experiences for later life, the importance of Eros in human motivation, and the dynamic interplay, including conflict, between the conscious and unconscious parts of the mind.

RJ: Do you think Freud is still a relevant thinker for the twenty-first century?

SK: In fact, that is true of him now more than, say, twenty to thirty years ago. I have been giving a talk on the Rebirth of Freud during the last couple of years, showing how recent developments in neurosciences and experimental psychology are validating many of the Freudian postulates while, of course, rejecting some. In fact, these modern developments go even further than Freud, by giving the unconscious a much larger role in mental life than Freud ever did. The unconscious may be more like an elephant, which you can't really control and which is mostly good-natured. It is not the headstrong horse of Freudian imagery, which can be controlled only with difficulty by the rider, the conscious part of the mind. The elephant is much stronger than the mahout and goes where it wants, though the mahout can nudge it in certain directions. There is certainly no point in getting into a fight with the elephant, a fight that the mahout is to bound lose. The neurosciences have also shown the vital importance of early childhood experiences in forming the neuronal pathways, the software of the brain. A lot of sifting will take place in psychoanalytic theories and models when it comes together with neurosciences, and it will be an exciting time. Personally, I agree with Erich Kandel, the 2000 Nobel Laureate for Medicine, that psychoanalysis is still the most coherent and intellectually satisfying view of the mind.

RJ: Will you describe yourself as a Freudian psychoanalyst or as a psychohistorian?

SK: I would describe myself as a cultural psychologist. I am a psychohistorian when I am working on a biography, which means that I take the cultural and historical context of an individual life more into account than some psychoanalysts may do.

RJ: Maybe that is why you write in our essay 'Culture in Psychoanalysis' that a 'there is no ideal analyst'.

SK: No, there are ideal analysts and there are ideal students, but no ideal gurus.

RJ: Can the analysis be done in English even if the mother tongue is any other language?

SK: It's not the ideal thing to do. A language other than your mother tongue lacks some basic emotions, no matter how rich your vocabulary and how perfect your grammar may be. This is because childhood feelings that are associated with the mother tongue are absent in the foreign language, which is usually learnt later in life.

RJ: So which language would you prefer to work with when you practise your therapy?

SK: In India, Punjabi and Hindi. English words naturally also occur in any Indian patient's discourse. Sometimes, they give clues to hidden emotions. For instance, whenever Indian patients talk about a parent's death, they use English words, and not Hindi, thus allowing them to maintain an emotional distance from the event and not be overwhelmed by sadness.

RJ: Do you have the same equivalences as in German, say for psychoanalytical and clinical practices. I know about Arabic and Persian. When we talk about the subconscious, then it has to be translated and that does not reflect the equivalence?

SK: For conscious and unconscious the equivalences in Hindi could be '*chetan*' and '*achetan*', but that is when one is writing and not in the practice of therapy. In clinical work, you try to avoid all abstractions. For instance, if anyone says in English that he feels hostile towards his father then I would want to know what lies behind the abstraction of the word 'hostile', whether he wants to kill, hit, strangle, or attack with a weapon. The use of abstractions encourages the defence of intellectualization.

RJ: Have you ever experienced any hostility from the Indian elite towards psychoanalysis or Freudian psychoanalysis?

SK: Yes.

RJ: Why is it so?

SK: The hostility emanates from certain kinds of people and not from all. We are talking about the intellectuals. Some Marxists see Freudian psychoanalysis, with its emphasis on the individual psyche, as an enemy of the Marxist worldview. Thus, once the vice-chancellor of Jawaharlal Nehru University (JNU), one of our premier centres of learning and also a bastion of Leftist thought, wanted me to join the faculty. But since the university did not have a Centre for Psychological Studies, my appointment could only be with the Centre for the Study of Social Systems. I was told that a few senior members of the Centre scuttled my appointment since I would have polluted the purity of the Ganga that issues from Marx's beard. But there are other Leftists and liberals who see psychoanalysis more as an ally in the emancipation of consciousness in the Indian context. Some Indian philosophers decry the materialism of psychoanalysis and its penchant for looking for clay feet in all gods while some others have a quarrel with its anti-religious stance. Psychoanalysis is an iconoclastic discipline. This means that it is a 'hermeneutics of suspicion' and would evoke hostility anywhere, and especially in India, where a large number of people subscribe to what I call the 'hermeneutics of idealization'.

RJ: Does it also have to do with the fact that the Freudian view on religion was influenced by the Judeo-Christian tradition and it's difficult for the Hindus to accept that?

SK: Very much so, since the religious critique of psychoanalysis is very far from a Hindu's religious experience. In fact, the International Psychoanalytic Association asks 10–12 people from the international community every year to revisit and analyse one of Freud's writings. I have recently done a piece on 'Reading *The Future of an Illusion* in Hindu India', wherein I have criticized Freud's ideas on religion from a Hindu perspective. As I said, I don't myself subscribe to all of Freud's ideas.

RJ: Well, is it because, as a Western-trained psychoanalyst, you have more intellectual preparation and also more tolerance. But some conservative Indians may exercise a complete rejection of the whole framework?

SK: Yes, but their rejection will be much more on the issue of the role of sexuality in human affairs than on the Freudian concept of religion.

Jung in the Mirror of Indians

RJ: Indians feel more inclined towards the theories of Jung than Freud.

SK: Yes, they do. I don't know whether you have read one of my essays called 'Encounters of the Psychological Kind: Freud, Jung and India'. Jung is a favourite among the Indian philosophers because they think that he appreciates and pays homage to Indian thought whereas Freud is a much more suspicious fellow. Yet, in case of some gurus I have met, they were more engaged by Freud because he is more challenging than Jung, who they felt did not offer them anything that they did not know before.

RJ: This is quite surprising because I remember that in the chapter on your encounter with Mataji, you say that she was surprised by the fact that you were a Freudian and not a Jungian, and she says that she prefers Jung to Freud.

SK: Yes, but she felt more challenged by Freud.

RJ: But have they read Freud?

SK: No, most of them know him second-hand, that is the sexual Freud. Some of them have also heard about the theories of Jung.

RJ: Maybe that is because Westerners have also been interested in people from the East, but Freud did not have much interest in people from the East. He was interested in old Egypt but that is not the whole of the East.

SK: True.

RJ: In your 'Encounters of the Psychological Kind', you mention that even if Jung admired India, his admiration for the Indian was for a civilized 'noble savage', possessing certain vital sensibilities, which the Westerner could be nostalgic about.

SK: Yes, and had he come to India today, he would have been terribly disappointed since there are only a couple of Jungians practicing in the country. I think there is one in Delhi and one in Bangalore. Jung does not hold surprises for anyone familiar with traditional Indian thought, both Hindu and Buddhist.

RJ: Maybe this is also what you have said to yourself. You have not used Jung as a theoretician?

SK: Nowadays, I am more interested in Jung but I feel no passion about Jung as I once felt for Freud. Jung is wonderfully wise yet he seems a little bloodless to me.

RJ: It is interesting that in various parts of his writings, Jung characterizes the Indian as feminine while the European represents the masculine?

SK: Both Jung and Freud were not free from the colonial context of their times, a context which demanded that Indians, a colonized people, needed to be perceived as soft, weak, and feminine. Both Jung and Freud were towering intellects but were caught in the web of history like any of us ordinary mortals. It just shows that no one is free from the spirit of the times in which he or she lives.

RJ: In your opinion, is it correct to see psychoanalysis through anti-colonial glasses as some Indian intellectuals in the 1960s did?

SK: I think they went too far. It's great to find a glass and look through it to discover something new but the process of looking has to be more acute. If you look through green glass, you will find that everything is green, but once you have discovered green, you should try to look for other colours.

The Art of being an Analyst in Indian Culture

RJ: Why do you think Indian psychoanalysts failed to produce enough clinical material in comparison to other cultures?

SK: There aren't many Indian analysts today who also write. The clinical material was produced by an earlier generation. That was the time when some of them were interested in the issue of psychoanalysis and its application to the Indian cultural milieu and Indian patients. But all such writings are mostly produced when you have colleagues who are interested in such discussions. That was true of the first generation of Indian analysts but is much less true today. Why do it when there is no demand or push for it?

RJ: Have you ever felt any kind of marginality about psychoanalysis among the Indian elites?

SK: Yes, but luckily I often went abroad for giving talks or on visiting professorships and encountered a great deal of interest and valuable feedback on my writings.

RJ: It's difficult, as you say, to practise a science which wants people to be autonomous.

SK: That is the most difficult part of practicing in India as your psychoanalytic worldview is always in opposition to the society's norms and values, starting with those of the patient's family. They say, 'What are you doing to my son/daughter?' So, there is always pressure of that kind on the analyst, but if you don't follow the analytic ideal of the individual having increased choices, then you aren't doing psychoanalysis but something else.

RJ: Did your family and friends accept you when you turned to psychoanalysis?

SK: I would not have become a psychoanalyst if I was not sure about my family's ultimate support in whatever I chose to do. My father was doubtful in the beginning but once I had decided, he accepted it wholeheartedly. Since he himself was an academic at heart, he was more interested in what I was writing and encouraged me to write more. Without that kind of support, I don't think becoming an analyst and a writer would have been possible for me.

RJ: They considered you as an eccentric in your family?

SK: Yes, they had thought that one day I would be the MD of a company. But my father told me later that when I was in Germany and we were having long-distance discussions through letters on changing my career, he had laughed when I wrote to him that I could not imagine spending the rest of my life selling tyres—with due apologies to the MD of Dunlop, India.

RJ: Being a psychoanalyst in Indian society is like being a homosexual or being part of a marginalized minority.

SK: It was akin to being marginalized only because people didn't know what it was all about. Everyone knows about homosexuals but not about psychoanalysts. Now, thirty years later, people know a little more about psychoanalysis due to newspaper and other media coverage, but even today, the knowledge of psychoanalysis among many intellectuals is limited to what I would call 'rumours about Freud'.

RJ: I remember that when I was in jail in Iran, one of my jail keepers asked me if I was a philosopher and he added that for him, being a philosopher meant that one is a lunatic. Did you ever have a similar experience?

SK: Well, no. I was more like a witch doctor but one who had the prestige of Western medicine behind him.

RJ: Do you think Indian universities are competent enough to impart psychoanalytic training to students?

SK: A beginning has been made. We have a Centre of Psychoanalytic Studies at Delhi University (DU). I am not sure how much support it has from the rest of the academic community, but it is a start. It is not for training students to become analysts but to familiarize them with the discipline, and I am told it attracts many students from other academic streams apart from psychology.

RJ: Were you interested in teaching psychoanalysis?

SK: I would have been if there had been an opportunity when I lived in Delhi.

RJ: So you do like to see your work also as academic work?

SK: Yes.

The Role of the Sacred

RJ: Allan Watts in *Psychotherapy: East and West* says that, 'Eastern religions are thinly veiled psychotherapy'. Do you agree with him?

SK: Yes. Eastern religion is a very broad concept, and perhaps he meant Buddhism and Hinduism. If he means that the guru–shishya relationship, in the Eastern religions is analogous to the analyst–analysand relationship, then I tend to agree with him. Their theoretical basis, though, is different. Psychoanalysis lays stress on the origins of human life while Eastern religions are more concerned about ends. They also differ on what the human potentials are, with psychoanalysis being more pessimistic than the religious traditions. But as far as healing is concerned, the defining moment of both is the relationship: guru–disciple in one case and analyst–analysand in the other

RJ: There are many people in the West today who look back at the role of the sacred in the healing sciences. You have written in the introduction of your book, *Shamans, Mystics and Doctors*, that in your experiences with the Indian healers and healing traditions, you were often aware of a general feeling of ambivalence, which came from your being Western-trained. Why this ambivalence?

SK: I was trained in being suspicious as to how much 'sacred' there is in what is touted as sacred and how much of it is really pretence—with an emphasis on the latter. My ambivalence remained but my own emphasis shifted from a denial of the sacred in the healing traditions to an acceptance of it, if only partially.

RJ: How would you define the sacred? Would you describe it as the 'noumenal' as Rudolf Otto did or would you analyse it differently?

SK: Otto's noumenal probably refers to the heights of the sacred. There are so many other, more ordinary moments when you are touched by something outside yourself. These are the moments which Mirza Ghalib, the great Urdu poet, refers to when he says, 'My thoughts come to me/From somewhere Beyond/When Ghalib is attuned/To the music of the stars.' One can come up on this sudden feeling of connectedness wherein the self is temporarily absent in many different contexts: in nature, in making love, while listening to a particular piece of music, or watching a mother feeding her baby. All these moments have a touch of the sacred.

RJ: Which takes you to the essence of being a human being?

SK: Yes.

RJ: Actually this is what Schopenhauer used to say about music, that it is the direct manifestation of the noumenal.

SK: Yes, I agree.

RJ: When one reads your book, *Shamans, Mystics and Doctors*, one is struck by the overwhelming role that the large number of healers exercise in India today, and the role of the 'alternative therapeutics' in Indian culture. Are they authenthic?

SK: Yes, most of them are, but as I said, you need not be authentic to be a guru or healer as long as your students or patients are authentic.

RJ: You mean that it is the patient who makes the healer and not the other way round?

SK: Exactly. As long as the healer doesn't disturb the patient's inward journey through some kind of inauthentic actions, that is, as long as he provides a secure, 'holding' environment, the healing will work. Of course, if the healer can drive the process forward through his own authenticity, the healing will be faster. But one need not touch the height of authenticity to be a healer.

RJ: This is very Freudian as you are talking about healers who are listening rather than talking. But my perception of an Indian guru is of somebody who is always talking to an audience unlike the Freudian idea where the doctor listens.

SK: Actually, the guru's words are the least important part of what is happening between him and his listeners. If you listen to what he is saying, it is mostly banal and repetitive. Words are only the medium through which people are receiving the feelings of being completely accepted by the guru, of being safe, and of the guru's indefinable essence, his charisma, if you will. Once a discourse is finished, people generally forget what the guru had said.

RJ: So it's just the presence, which is important.

SK: Yes, the talking presence, the listening presence, or whatever.

RJ: Did you ever try to learn these alternative therapeutics?

SK: As I said, there was not much to learn because the systems behind the different therapeutics, their classifications of disorders, their conceptions of pathogenic agents, their degrees of sophistication—all these are secondary to the establishing and deepening of a therapeutic relationship.

RJ: Have you ever had patients with strong spiritual beliefs who needed to see a *shaman*?

SK: Yes, but I had them later. I had some earlier, too, but they did not bring out their spiritual beliefs in psychotherapy because the unconscious need of a patient to be loved by the analyst is so great that he would excise parts of his self which he believes the analyst will not welcome. So I never saw the spiritual side of my patients in the beginning, since I was pretty much an orthodox Freudian with little sympathy for religion or spirituality. Later, when I became more open to the spiritual side, these beliefs were also articulated by patients. You know, that is why they say a Freudian analyst's patients always dream Freudian dreams while a Jungian analyst will always get Jungian dreams from his patients.

A Guru Culture

RJ: Did you have a cabin when you started your practice?

SK: Yes, I had a separate room in my house.

RJ: What did it look like?

SK: A typical Freudian one, with bookshelves lining the walls, a couch and my chair behind the couch.

RJ: Was it accepted by the Indians?

SK: The Indians accepted it easily since I was a guru in their cultural imagination and whatever arrangement the guru thinks is right is accepted unquestioningly by Indians.

RJ: You said at some point in your book, *Shamans, Mystics and Doctors*, that you are a Hindu after all, and traditionally do not seek a synthesis of opposites but are content to keep each as it is. I found this quite interesting. Do you believe that we always ought to have diversity but never seek its synthesis?

SK: Yes, but this is true not only of me as I also found this attitude in many of my academic colleagues. Initially, I thought that this was because they wanted to avoid conflict but it is more about an easier acceptance of a co-existence of differences.

RJ: Many charlatans and fake analysts also practise the alternative therapeutic. How would you distinguish between the authentic Ayurvedic therapy and healing culture, on one hand, and the inauthentic ones, on the other? Would it be enough to ensure whether they are embedded in symbolic central structures of the universe or not? Do we need something else to test their authenticity?

SK: It is very difficult to test the authenticity of anyone. What is authentic to one is inauthentic to another, and vice versa. For instance, some believe that Osho Rajneesh, was a completely inauthentic and wild guru. Others think that he was the greatest guru of modern times and absolutely authentic. I do not doubt either and accept both the versions.

RJ: You also have individuals like Deepak Chopra.

SK: I would say the same about him. I can make judgements about banality, but not about authenticity.

RJ: We were talking about the role of a psychoanalyst to make people autonomous, to get back to the concept of self, which is so important in the West. What would you say is the difference between the Indian and the Western concept of autonomy?

SK: Simply put, the Western notion is of a self that is encapsulated. And if the Western self has a location that lies inside the body, in the brain, then the Indian self is much more open and strongly influenced by its surroundings. You may picture it like a TV set receiving signals from the universe, whereas the Western self occurs as receiving signals from the neurons firing in the brain. The Indian self is more at the junction of the body and the universe than in the case of the modern Western conception of the self.

RJ: Is the Indian injunction of 'know thyself' related to the same self as the one referred to by the Socratic vision?

SK: No, they are two completely different ways of knowing the self. The Socratic injunction is to know your biographical self whereas the Indian injunction refers to a metaphysical self.

RJ: Is there a critical examination like the Socratic vision?

SK: Critical examination, yes, but not in the Socratic vision. In the *Dhyana* tradition, the ten *Mahavakyas* keep on boring deeper and deeper into the nature of the self. They keep on peeling one layer of the onion after another and asking oneself to examine whether what remains is the self.

RJ: Does the concept of autonomy appear as unnatural to Indian culture or not?

SK: It does. Not that the idea of the completely autonomous individual, like the *sanyasi* who has freed himself from all worldly relationships and bonds, does not exist in India. However, it is an idea that is not mainstream and it does not apply or appeal to most people. In India, the opposite of autonomy is seen to be connectedness, which is highly valued, while in the West, the opposite of autonomy is generally thought as dependence, which has very negative connotations. In any case, even in the West, pure autonomy is a myth.

RJ: In the West, we talk about the autonomy of politics, but in India someone like Gandhi talked about the spiritualization of politics in opposition to the politicization of religion, which does not mean much to the Westerner as an individual who lives in the secularized world of the twenty-first century. For an Indian, this understanding comes more easily.

SK: Yes, probably there would be a different understanding. One would think that Indians, in spite of their contemporary experience of a completely amoral politics still believe that politics without moral values, which may be seen as a part of spirituality, is bad. I don't think this comes close to Gandhi's view of spiritualization of politics, which implied a politics driven by love and not only by moral values.

RJ: I asked you this question because I wanted to bring out the concept of holism and individualism, which is so important in Indian culture. Would it be correct to say that India is a non-individualistic culture, which is today experiencing forms of individualism?

SK: Yes, I think it would be correct to say so. I would also add that it is a non-individualistic culture where many more people are experiencing and discovering the pleasures of individuality, and are often getting carried away by them. Individualism, of course, also has its negative side. I often got the feeling that my Western patients suffered from excesses of individualism where there is a feeling of isolation and lack of connection.

Living with Cultural Schizophrenia

RJ: Doesn't it create a kind of cultural schizophrenia for an Indian to have, at the same time, a holistic view of the self and also to enjoy the pleasure of individualism?

SK: Well, Indians do not need to integrate opposites as much as people of some other cultures need to. Indians do not experience cognitive dissonance while holding two contradictory views to the same degree as in the West, and can postpone making choices for a longer time.

RJ: They do create tension and conflict, at least at the level of family structures?

SK: Yes, that they do.

RJ: I refer to Satyajit Ray's movie *Mahanagar* wherein he portrays a woman who goes out of the house to work, which destroys her relationship with her husband completely.

SK: Well, that is certainly true of modern India wherein the idea of a woman working outside the house has been completely accepted at an intellectual level but still creates emotional conflicts for the family.

RJ: How can one juggle with that? I come from a traditional society. In the Middle East, traditions are very different, but there has been a lot of violence because of the encounter of the traditional with the modern.

SK: These issues are not resolved that easily. But people juggle with the modern and traditional in their lives and chart a course without violent turbulence causing the ship to capsize.

RJ: I am very surprised when you say that they always try to juggle and find a solution by themselves without any kind of violence, which means that they adjust with the encounter of the modern with the tradition.

SK: It means in the sense of postponing certain kind of choices.

RJ: You mean putting it at the back of your mind?

SK: Yes, saying that I will deal with the difficult choice later, at some other point of time. For example, a young girl suffering at the hands of her mother-in-law will say silently to herself, 'Let me wait till I become a mother-in-law and get the power I now lack.' Or someone saying, 'My child will have all that I have missed out in my own childhood.' Keeping a dream alive, postponing gratification rather than cutting off a part of the self, is a solution that is adopted most of the time. Sometimes you have to make your choices in the present like the woman in the movie you talked about. Such choices are difficult to make and most of the time they are made in the interest of the solidarity and welfare of the family, and individual rebellion is rare.

RJ: Even at the level of young people?

SK: Yes.

RJ: But you could never have what I would call a 'James Dean syndrome' in India?

SK: No, we don't have such a syndrome at the collective level. We have tension between the generations but not open conflict, a stretching of the bond between generations, but rarely an open break.

RJ: Suppose a homosexual comes to you with his problems. How would you solve his problems and how does his family solve it in India?

SK: I will help him solve it in the sense that if he is a homosexual, then he should learn to accept or embrace his homosexuality, but he does not have to assert his homosexual identity openly if he does not want to. He should come to terms with and get a measure of ease with his sexuality. Generally, in the family there is a tradition of benign neglect. In other words, the homosexuality is ignored as long as the person does not rub it in the family's face so that other people come to know about it. The parents are more concerned about what others would say if they found out about their son's or daughter's homosexuality and less about the deviant sexuality itself. I remember one male homosexual patient asking me whether I had a lesbian patient whom he could marry so that both the families would be satisfied. After marriage, he could do his own thing and she could do hers, but for their parents and the rest of society, it would suffice that they were a married couple.

Part III

Between Private and Public

Modern India and Traditional Morality

RJ: In India, do we have a rupture between the private and the public?

SK: Very much so. For instance, *izzat* or honour of the family, which is more a public than a private construct, becomes extremely important because what happens to izzat is not only important for your own self-esteem and the way it influences your life, but is also important for the fate of your family; a loss of izzat may mean that your sister and brother will not find suitable spouses.

RJ: So it's not an individual morality but a communitarian one?

SK: Yes.

RJ: So you always have to keep that aspect in your mind when you are dealing with an Indian patient to whom the idea of community is more important than the idea of the self?

SK: Yes, but I have to make him realize that the individual part of him is as important as the communitarian one and then leave him to make his own choices in different situations.

RJ: And the choice is usually communitarian.

SK: Mostly, but not always. In the case of the homosexual patient I was talking about, he decided that he would go and settle down in the USA, where he could live out his sexuality more openly but not without the certain risk of weakening his emotional links with his family.

RJ: How is it that homosexuality is seen as a deviation in India and yet you have the transvestites who are so easily accepted in Indian society? Is it because one is culturally oriented while the other finds itself outside the traditional world?

SK: It is because procreation is the most important task for a person in India and anyone who refuses to procreate is looked down upon. Having sex with a partner of the same sex is frowned upon because there is no chance of procreation in such a coupling. It is not the sex part which is disturbing, not what you are doing but with whom you are doing it, that becomes vital for society's acceptance or rejection. Transvestites are accepted but also pitied because they cannot procreate and are thus deficient in a fundamental sense.

RJ: Not being married and not having a child is also seen as a bad thing in India.

SK: Yes, whoever cannot produce an offspring is a failure as a human being.

RJ: So the Indian society, like the Mesopotamian societies, is based on the idea of fertility.

SK: Yes, sexuality is not a sin but procreation is a great virtue.

RJ: And yet the concept of non-fertility is completely solved in Europe, which means sexuality is more important to them than fertility?

SK: Yes, which means that Europeans have largely divorced fertility from sexuality but here in India that is not the case.

The Fear of Sexuality

RJ: In India, as you have described in your book, *Intimate Relations*, that sex is both loved and feared. In which way is it loved and in which way is it feared?

SK: The fear is one of losing sexual fluids, which leads to physical, mental, and spiritual weakness. As you know, in the Indian hydraulics of sexuality, the celibate's semen increases, which makes for spiritual enlightenment. These are Tantric ideas, very much in the underground but quite influential. Semen is also considered to be the source of intellect and memory, so any loss of semen is feared. The love of sexuality is, of course, the fulfilment of a universal desire for completion through the union with the other sex as much as for attaining the summit of pleasure.

RJ: In India, traditionally, sexuality and morality have always been fused together. Do you think there has been a shift vis-à-vis sexual morality in the Indian society?

SK: I think it is shifting towards a more liberal direction. It started in the upper class elite in the metropolises, and then spread, through the media, to the smaller towns. But this shift towards a freer sexual expression, especially among women, is also accompanied by a strong movement in the opposite direction in some sections of Indian society.

RJ: When you say 'elite', do you mean the Western-oriented elite?

SK: I mean that.

RJ: Not the middle class?

SK: No, the middle class is still quite conservative.

RJ: Was sex always taboo in India?

SK: Sex has always has been a part of a dialectic between asceticism and eroticism in India. For instance, eroticism seems to have been ascendant between the fourth and twelfth centuries, as reflected in literature, temple sculptures, and so on, of this period. Then a gradual change began wherein the ascetic view of man's strivings got the upper hand and which looked at sex as a subverter of its ideals. The priestly, ascetic discourse, combined with the Puritanism of the British colonial masters, has been dominant for the last three centuries though the equation between asceticism and eroticism seems to be changing once again in favour of the latter.

RJ: What are your ideas on the psychodynamics of sexuality in today's world? I am talking about the twenty-first century. In the West, people talk more and more about individual rights and it is present not only at the economic level but also at the level world of faith. For example, the fact that priests could be homosexuals or lesbians has created a lot of tension among the followers of the Roman Catholic Church. It seems that that sexual discourse has changed a lot.

SK: Yes, in the West, sex seems to have emancipated itself completely from any moral considerations. The danger of a sexuality without inhibitions or prohibitions is that, while escaping the ice of morality it falls into the fire of pure indulgence. Sex becomes divorced from intimacy or love. It becomes a search for sensation, for pleasure, and I believe an addiction to sensation is as dangerous to a person's emotional well-being as moralistic prohibitions.

The Ganesha Complex

RJ: Do you believe in certain moral norms in human sexual relations?

SK: Yes, sexuality is the procreative fire which a person can take lightly only at his own peril. I can't separate sexuality from love and intimacy. Without love, there is no possibility of self-transcendence in the sexual embrace. The greatest promise of sex lies not in the pleasure it provides but in those rare moments of transcendence, which are not possible without a loving connectedness to the partner. Without love, sex is just a joint masturbation, a masturbation *à deux*.

RJ: Sexuality doesn't work in India as it works in the West, and so you suggest the Ganesha complex, which is also the hegemonic development of the narrative of the male self in Hindu India. How do you distinguish between the Oedipus complex and the Ganesh complex?

RJ: The Oedipus complex is about the son's rivalry with the father in relation to the mother and his fantasized parricide. In the Ganesha complex, the son withdraws from this sexual rivalry by renouncing sexual activity. In the *Mahabharata*, for instance, Bhishma and Puru are examples of the Ganesha complex.

RJ: It also goes back to the idea of an ideal woman in India. An ideal woman is defined by her relation with her husband and her sons, and being a good daughter or wife.

SK: The father–son rivalry in India is also very different from that in Western mythology. In Indian imagination, that is, in its folk tales and legends, it is not the son who is jealous of the father for possessing the mother, but the father who is envious of the son because of the mother's emotional investment in her son.

RJ: So it has mostly to do with the image of the mother in the Indian family, the husband–wife bond is not as strong as the mother–son bond? The maternal images that we have in India also have a darker side in Indian mythology, which are the hideous goddesses. How do they go together—the hideous and the brighter parts?

SK: The hideous mother is one who is so involved in the son that she smothers him with her love, leaving him with little room to become a man who functions independently of her. The image of the mother is both of a beneficient, nurturant goddess, and a darker, devouring one.

RJ: Is the maternal part more important than the paternal part in Indian sexuality?

SK: Yes, paternal gods are like the elder males of the family who are respected but who are remote from the day-to-day affairs of the family that concern the child, and are thus less important in the child's scheme of things than the women of the family, the various 'mothers'. In the hierarchical structure of the family, the eldest male may be the titular head but important decisions regarding daily life are taken by the female with the highest status.

RJ: In Ray's movie, *Devi*, members of a family and even neighbours attribute the status of a goddess to a woman who doesn't want it. She finds herself in a very peculiar and strange position. Is that common in Hindu culture?

SK: Yes, I won't say that the goddess status of women is quite common but many women do suffer under male idealizations, for instance, of being regarded as sexually pure. They are shackled by such idealizations and are not allowed to be normal human beings. Women are supposed to be self-sacrificing, pure, etc., and these male projections are certainly not very great as far as a woman is concerned.

RJ: Would you relate all the problems of dowry, and killings which follow, to the idealization of woman in India?

SK: I don't think there is much connection between the two.

RJ: Sati is forbidden by law. Is it related to that?

SK: The idea of sati is related to the male projection of a woman's complete devotion and faithfulness to one person, the husband, even after death. She becomes a goddess if she lives up to this idealization.

Hindu Myths and Sexuality

RJ: Would you say that Indian sexual exploration is still very much influenced by the Hindu myths?

SK: Yes, many of the gods are frankly sexual. Some like Indra and Kartikeya are cursed for their promiscuity. The most ascetic of sages rarely withstands the temptations put in his way by the god of desire while one of the great gods, Shiva, is both ascetic and erotic. Indian mythology is infused with sexuality in all its brilliant and vivid colours.

RJ: This implies the invocation of myths?

SK: Yes, myths are constantly invoked by people in their conversations, in television dramas, movies, plays, dance dramas, and so on. As compared to the West, where myths are of interest mainly to the mythologist, myths are very much alive in India. Here, they are invoked not only to address sexual dilemmas but to provide resolutions for many of life's problems. I remember that once I was travelling in the hills. It was just a day after the Emergency had been declared. I stopped for tea at a roadside teashop where people were discussing Indira Gandhi's radio statement giving her reasons for imposing the Emergency. One man was very vehement in his opposition and was saying that she was completely lying. Another, her supporter, alluding to a story in the *Mahabharata*, shut him up by saying that in politics even Lord Krishna had lied.

RJ: Does the existence of charismatic politics in India, say the charisma of the Nehru dynasty, have to do with the representation of myth in Indian politics?

SK: Yes, some outstanding leaders succeed in connecting with the mythical imagination. He or she assumes a mythical status and their descendants too get some of that charisma attached to them. Even though Gandhi and Nehru have not been dead for a long time, they are already mythical figures. It's somewhat like anyone who has descended from the line of the Prophet is sacred.

RJ: How are the sexual and the erotic intertwined in *Bhakti* poetry?

SK: Bhakti poetry is very much like Sufi poetry wherein the erotic imagery is supposed to signify the union of a human being with God. The difference between the two is that whereas Sufi poetry conceives of god as the Beloved, Bhakti poetry is generally feminine in its orientation where god is the lover and the human being the beloved. In the Radha–Krishna poems and songs, human beings identify with Radha's passionate love for Krishna, and a devotee seeks to recreate Radha's responses within himself or herself. My impression is that Radha's passionate and erotic love for Krishna, raised to its highest intensity, is not an allegory for religious passion but is religious passion. In Bhakti, I believe, you do not need to make a distinction or choose between the religious and the erotic.

RJ: The Muslims in India seem to have taken it from the Persian Sufis.

SK: Yes.

RJ: Which you don't find among the Arabs?

SK: Yes, and I wonder why. Maybe it's because of the idea that you can't unite with a figure like Allah who evokes so much awe. If you conceive of the Divine as someone who is near you, then you can have an erotic relationship with the Divine. But if you consider Him as a distant figure, as a strict, even if loving, father of whom one is in awe, then you cannot have erotic feelings towards god. The Arab conception of Allah may be seen more in terms of distance and awe than nearness and love.

RJ: I think Muslims in India have been more influenced by the Hindus. I am talking about the middle class. They can listen to Sufi ghazals at the same level at which they listen to Hindustani vocal music. It comes very naturally to them.

SK: Yes.

RJ: What is the enigma here? The line of separation exists in other Muslim cultures but not in India?

SK: In both the Sufi ghazal and Hindustani vocal music, it is the feeling towards the object that is important. In a sense, both signify the music of love.

RJ: Great saints in all religious traditions, have used sex as a metaphor to describe a union with the beloved, whether it be Christianity, Islam, or Hinduism. Would you say that mystical ecstasy and sexual ecstasy are complementary to each other?

SK: I think most people have experienced sexual but not mystical ecstasy and thus the former is the only signpost we have for the latter. But it is not sexual ecstasy but the small moment of silence after the orgasm when the two bodies have become separate but the souls are still united which, I believe, is akin to the unio mystica.

RJ: But we have this idea that mysticism is a never-ending quest after its own perfection. Do you agree with that?

SK: Mysticism for me implies the exhausting of all our potentials, the emptiness of the stage when the riveting performance of desire ends.

RJ: In your novel *Ecstasy*, which is loosely based on the historical relationship between Ramakrishna and Vivekananda, what were you looking for? Why didn't you take, for example, Aurobindo or Tagore?

SK: I chose them because Ramakrishna's is an older, traditional form of spirituality, completely disinterested in social issues, while Vivekananda represents a more modern spirituality that is involved with our social and political worlds. Both Aurobindo and Tagore are very modern. Ramakrishna was not modern at all and yet he became the guru of an icon of Indian modernity, Vivekananda. How? The desire to find out why Vivekananda chose such a person as his guru and the interplay of tradition and modernity through their personas was something that interested me.

RJ: Do you think that it is possible to take Tagore's methodology and then apply it to Indian sexuality?

SK: I don't think so. I need to explore the dialectic and the conflict between the spirit and the flesh to write a novel. I do not know enough of Tagore's inner conflicts.

The World of the *Kamasutra*

RJ: Why did you need a new translation of the *Kamasutra,* and what were the flaws in the old Burton translation?

SK: Each era evolves its own language, and therefore, needs a new translation of an old classic. The older Burton translation also had certain limitations. There is a degree of Orientalism in the translation. For instance, he uses the terms *lingam* and *yoni* for male and female sexual organs, respectively, which do not occur in the original text. Lingam and yoni are signifiers of Shiva and his spouse, respectively, and their use in the *Kamasutra* can be deeply offensive to a believing Hindu. There are also some mistranslations in the Burton text, which changes the whole meaning of a passage. There are errors in the translation; like that a woman should not scold a man when he has an affair with another woman while the original text says that she should. Burton also uses indirect speech whereas in the text the speech is direct. He also pads the translation by borrowing from a commentary written 800 years after the original text. There is also an underplaying of the woman's agency in sex.

RJ: Did Burton incorporate Victorian morality into his translation?

SK: No, I must say that Victorian morality is not there in the translation. Orientalism is an issue with his translation, but not Victorianism.

RJ: What is interesting in the *Kamasutra* is that it gives voice to Indian women, who are quoted by the author in direct speech. Is that the originality of the text?

SK: Yes, it is. Also there is much more sympathy for the woman. For example, the *Kamasutra* is the only ancient Indian text which says that a love marriage is the highest form of marriage, and that if a woman is not satisfied with her husband, then she should seek satisfaction outside marriage. In that sense, the *Kamasutra* is representative of a very modern morality.

RJ: Would you place the *Kamasutra* in the same category as the *Arthashastra*?

SK: Yes, the *Kamasutra* was influenced by the structure of the *Arthashastra*.

RJ: So it's a guide to love and pleasure.

SK: A guide to sexual pleasure.

RJ: If we want to teach the *Kamasutra* in psychology or philosophy classes, what will be the concerns in today's world?

SK: The important aspect would be to emphasize women's agency in sexuality. The other would be that eroticism requires lightness and playfulness, and that we are truly serious only when we play.

RJ: I remember that you said in an interview that if Vatsyayana was alive today, he would be the publisher of *Playboy Magazine* rather than a pornographer.

SK: Yes.

RJ: Does that mean that *Playboy Magazine* is considered as a more serious way of approaching eroticism in today's world, rather than merely sexual pleasure? Is the *Kamasutra* also a reflection on sexuality?

SK: Yes, a reflection and an elaboration.

RJ: The style is also very interesting, written in condensed prose without entirely being in prose.

SK: Yes, that is because of the oral transmission of knowledge in ancient India. The text had to be very concise so that it could be easily memorized, and one could elaborate and comment on the passages while teaching it.

RJ: Who read the *Kamasutra* at that time?

SK: The court society, the rich merchants, and others of the leisured class. I will say the same kind of people who read it today, with the addition of young students who keep it hidden in a brown bag and read it in the toilet.

RJ: Why in a brown bag?

SK: Because it's still a forbidden text. If it is found in your room, then the family is not going to be too happy about it.

RJ: In what way is Western eroticism different from the *Kamasutra* philosophy?

SK: I will say, in its lack of playfulness and in its complete divorce of eroticism from moral concerns. Although the *Kamasutra* elaborates on every kind of sexual situation, at the end of each elaboration, it would always take a position on what is morally right and what is not. Today, if we read magazines and watch late night programmes on TV, we see a complete divorce between morality and sexuality. Sex is no longer erotic but pornographic.

RJ: There is also the idea of ascetic celibacy, which is so important in Indian culture and totally absent in Western culture. I mean the *Brahmacharya*?

SK: Yes.

RJ: Many in the West forget that in the *Kamasutra*, there is a lot of dharma along with *artha* and moksha. How do you describe the work of these three concepts in Indian sexuality?

SK: Dharma, artha, and *kama* are the three chief aims of life and they all go together in achieving the final goal of moksha. Each aim of life has a separate *shastra* devoted to it. The shastras dealing with each aim are separate but also intimately connected. For instance, sexuality must be within the framework of dharma. Indeed, the caste system of the *Dharmashastra* is also reflected in the *Kamasutra*. There is no democracy there. It forbids a man to have sexual relation with a low-caste woman or with a tribal woman because they have no idea of eroticism. It also talks about sexual actions which are possible but should not be attempted, and which have to do with the Dharmashastra's notions of pollution and purity. Sex in the mouth is OK but anal sex is completely disapproved of since it is polluting.

RJ: And the concept of power or artha.

SK: Artha, of course, makes eroticism possible since the erotic life depicted in the *Kamasutra* needs a lot of money and leisure.

RJ: As you write in your novel, *The Ascetic of Desire*, the power of sexual desire frees the lover from all past lives. Does this mean that one crosses the gulf from the human to the divine in the sexual act?

SK: I prefer to see it as the basic message of the *Kamasutra*.

RJ: In your introduction written with Wendy Doniger, you say that the *Kamasutra* has attained a classical status because it is basically about unchangeable human attributes such as love, seduction, and other similar things. Is this the message of the *Kamasutra*?

SK: Yes, one of its messages.

Part IV

The Message of India

A Loving Critical Eye

RJ: When you write a novel, how much of your psychoanalysis experience is involved in it?

SK: If I have involved my psychoanalysis experience in the writing of my fiction, then that has not been a conscious undertaking but has happened as an aspect of who I am.

RJ: If you have to do the classification, how would you distinguish your fictional works from your theoretical studies?

SK: There is a distinction between the two in terms of their writing. One is more imaginative and connotative while the other, the theoretical, is discursive. But since I am the one who is doing both kinds of writing, there will certainly be some commonalities. Sexuality and spirituality, for instance, have been common themes in both kinds of writing.

RJ: How does the inspiration come in choosing a theme?

SK: Themes come unsought. After I have done a lot of reading, something interesting comes up and I may choose to write an essay on it first. I wrote an article on Gandhi once, as I also did on

Ramakrishna. Later, in the fullness of time, they also entered my fictional world.

RJ: So the idea of the flesh and the spirit has been there in your mind for 30–40 years as a permanent thread?

SK: Yes.

RJ: But did you ever want to write a study on non-violence in relation to what you read of Gandhi?

SK: No, Gandhi's spirit, his struggle, the brahmacharya part of it, and the spiritual goals he set for himself interested me more.

RJ: Do you still feel close to Erikson's methodology with which you started in the beginning?

SK: It has become a part of my working life, a part of how I think about people and events, and I am no longer conscious of it as a method.

RJ: Are you aware of your audience?

SK: I don't write for any audience that is not already in my head: a few friends and dear ones, my father, my mentor—some dead, others still alive.

RJ: Do you practise the art of writing on a systematic basis?

SK: No.

RJ: Would you say that your work is rooted very much in the Indian experience, say mystical and historical times?

SK: Yes, I am quite Indian in that way.

RJ: You live with both of them; Indian history and the myths.

SK: Yes, and I don't make hard and fast distinctions between the two.

RJ: Your time and space are both mythical and historical?

SK: Yes.

RJ: Maybe your isolation in Goa helps you a lot?

SK: Yes, though I wouldn't call it isolation but solitude.

RJ: Does your experience with the West help you to look at Indian culture and society with a loving critical eye?

SK: I am very critical of contemporary India with my countrymen when I am in India, and I am very loving towards India when I am abroad, defending Indian ways and idiosyncrasies.

A New Indian Struggle

RJ: What are the issues in the West which you defend in India?

SK: In India, I have strong views on the human rights of women, whether they be Hindu, Muslim, or of any other religion. I don't believe in the cultural relativity of human rights. Outside, I will defend cultural relativity, culturally specific ways of looking at the world, the contextual sensitivity of Indians, and so on. I seem to be more on the side of cultural relativity outside India and of universality inside.

RJ: You take the message of India outside when you are writing in German, in newspapers, or when you are teaching in France?

SK: Yes.

RJ: You said in an interview that change will never come unless you try to understand a problem in different ways. It means that you think of change and also look at the Indian problem in a different way. And the same applies for international issues?

SK: Yes, I like to think of a problem from many different viewpoints to change my own perceptions of it. Even from the viewpoint of those who will reflexively reject my thoughts. I believe in Nietzsche's observation that one should look for wisdom in the mind of one's opponent.

RJ: Have you ever been interested in taking a more political role in Indian society?

SK: No.

RJ: You were a radical student when you were young?

SK: But that was because of my own psychological needs. At that time, I thought that I was working to change the outer world but discovered later that it was actually to change my inner one.

RJ: Are you interested in politics?

SK: No, because I think I cannot be manipulative and Machiavellian as one kind of politics, the dominant kind today, demands. I am too idealistic for that. I cannot also subscribe to the idealism of another kind of politics that animates some of Indian civil society; I am too suspicious of human motives for that.

RJ: Will you feel at ease if I ask you questions about politics?

SK: Yes.

RJ: I am really interested in knowing your point of view about the evolution of politics in India from Nehru to Gandhi. Do you think it is going down?

SK: Absolutely.

RJ: Has it become corrupted?

SK: Corrupted and unbelievably venal. The idea of being involved and in service of something larger than yourself has disappeared.

RJ: What happened? Does India still remain the land of Gandhi, Tagore, and Nehru?

SK: I think what happened was that the days of Gandhi and Tagore were exceptional. Politics under colonialism was attuned to the cause of freedom and the building of a nation. It was not limited to satisfying the interests of one's family, village, or caste. It was more universal than local, and that was inspiring as were the leaders who articulated its vision. Once the pressure of foreign domination disappeared and also those leaders passed away, we came back to Indian life as usual, dominated by the age-old values of familism and casteism. The days of Gandhi and Tagore were exceptional both because of the men and the circumstances in which they lived.

RJ: If you start with the first Indian encounters with modernity, people like Ram Mohan Roy, and later on with Gokhale and Tagore, we can see that they all had something important to say in favour and against modernity. But today whether on the side of the Congress Party or the BJP or even among the followers of Gandhi, nobody has anything interesting to say. Indian elites don't seem to have the same type of exchanges. Was it the readings of people like Tagore and Gandhi which was exceptional?

SK: Roy, Tagore, Nehru, and Gandhi had something relevant to contribute because the issue of tradition versus modernity was still relatively new and there was much to say, especially since the votaries of tradition were both vociferous and vigorous. Now the debate has gone on for a long time and there isn't much scope left for fresh ideas. The diehard traditionalists have also disappeared and the salvaging of some, but not all, of the Indian cultural traditions in the country's modernity project, seems to have become a consensus.

India and its Discontents

RJ: In the Middle East, we had our own encounters with modernity. But what interests me in India is that despite its encounter with modernity it remained a traditional culture. How was the reconciliation between modernity and tradition done in Indian culture? How could Indians be modern up to some point and yet remain traditional without losing their identity?

SK: For one, there has been a long tradition in India of absorbing influences coming from outside and dealing with them in a creative manner. Indians have never completely absorbed nor completely rejected foreign ideas and influences. They have digested them in a process of assimiliation and re-creation. Modernity, or at least modernity in parts, has been welcomed by even the most fanatical of Hindu revivalists. For instance, they have always been enthusiastic about the technological aspects of modernity and even some of its legal framework. So modernity has not come in a bundle but has been disaggregated. Yes, to some part of modernity, and no, to others.

RJ: Which values of modernity were wrong, among these that were taken by the Indian norms or practices or ways of thinking?

SK: Individualism for instance, especially its narcissistic extreme, the 'looking out for number one'. Extreme individualism is as pernicious as is the extreme familism toward which Indians are inclined. The movement towards individualism, so evident among the elite during the Nehruvian era, seems to be again declining again.

RJ: Do you think India can one day become a non-hierarchical society?

SK: One day I hope so, but I think that will take a long time. Legally, yes, but the disappearance of the hierarchical approach to social relations in the mind will take a while.

RJ: It is very difficult to disturb the mental get-up?

SK: Yes.

RJ: Is that one of the ways in which Indians are the most undemocratic in the world?

SK: One of the world's most undemocratic people living in the world's largest democracy.

RJ: Are you hopeful of the Indian youngsters?

SK: Yes.

RJ: Why, because of their approach to sexuality or morality?

SK: No, because they are young and take more chances with inherited values. They venture out more, both physically and intellectually. I admire this adventurousness which, however, does not weaken the younger generation's contact with tradition and the older generation.

The Art of Indianness

RJ: Do they manage to resist globalization? Where is their cultural sense of belongingness?

SK: When you look at the Indian diaspora, you see them clinging much more to Indian cultural traditions. In a sense, there is more Indianness among Indians who live in the heartlands of the globalized world.

RJ: Do you believe in the idea that one gets what one deserves? Today, young Indians want to engage in IT and business. They want to get the world and deserve the world. They think that the world is theirs and they just have to go and get it. Is it some kind of a new philosophy?

SK: Yes, that is the adventurous part. But you can venture out more easily if there is a safe harbour to return to, the harbour of family and its traditions.

RJ: I read your first book published with Kamla Chowdhry in the 1970s, which was on Indian youth. In this book you are very much concerned with the authority crisis in Indian society, which was translated into the spectacular violence on the streets. Do you think that the spirit of protest is still there?

SK: I think it is there in the resurgence of Naxalite insurgency, and other, less violent social protest movements. There are a lot of issues involved in these movements but part of their animation is the youthful spirit.

RJ: But other things have changed?

SK: Yes.

RJ: I remember that you said in your book that pre-marital sexual relations were exceptional among the college youth.

SK: Yes, that has not changed much, in spite of the media hype. As long as you have arranged marriages—and these marriages continue to be preferred by the young—the girls cannot afford to have a blot on their sexual reputation, which will diminish not only their own value in the marriage market but also that of their siblings. That fact acts as an inhibition in pre-marital sexual relations rather than any moral considerations.

RJ: So it happens only in urban areas?

SK: Yes, mostly in urban areas and mainly among the higher middle classes. For young men, it happens a great deal with sex workers.

RJ: How would you define Indianness in today's world?

SK: That is what I tried to do in my book, *The Indians*.

RJ: Yes, but if you have to define it in two words then how will you do that? Can I be an Indian?

SK: If you have 4–5 psychological traits, then you could be called an Indian. One is a high emphasis on connectedness to others, especially family and caste. Then, having a hierarchical vision of social relations, and a relativistic rather than an absolute way of thinking which, of course, can degenerate into the extreme of '*Sab chalta hai*!'—Anything goes!—will help in making you an Indian, as also a worldview and a moral framework articulated in the myths and legends of the epics.

RJ: Where will you put the concept of diversity in relation to Indianness? Is it important?

SK: I think too much emphasis has been paid to Indian diversity, perhaps also because of the anthropological way of thinking that became so pronounced in the last century, dazzling us with the surface differences among India's peoples. Diversity is one of the country's greatest resources. But diversity can also be divisive and the question arises as to whether the protection of this diversity does not need a framework to contain its centrifugal forces. Super-ordinate identities, like the Indian identity or Indianness, if they evolve with the mutual consent of various groups and are not imposed by force or diktat, dampen internal conflicts and are an antidote to divisiveness. This was and continues to be one of the important guiding impulses behind the search for a European identity that would end the conflicts between Europe's nations, or the beginnings of a search for an African identity. There are many other examples but the important point to note is that Indianness is not inimical to other cultural identities but, in fact, may ensure their survival. I am not talking of a unity but a search for harmony within India's diversity.

A Dialogue between Religion and Secularism

RJ: Many people outside India consider India solely as a Hindu culture. So they will not talk about harmony but about the differences in religions. Actually, there are two perceptions; one that Indians have of themselves, and the other that they are a part of the society called India, which is at times quite contradictory.

SK: Just because it has been appropriated by the Hindutva notion of the Sangh *parivar*, it should not blind us to the fact that Hindu culture is indeed the prominent strain in the cultural gene pool of India's peoples. Not that it has not changed over the centuries—as it certainly has—through its encounters with other cultures. I believe that the hierarchical vision of the Hindu eye, for instance, would have been much worse but for the encounter with Islam and its concept of brotherhood. On the other hand, Hindu culture has greatly influenced other religious cultures in India by introducing them to the 4–5 psychological features of Indianness which we just talked about. Thus, an Indian Muslim is quite different from an Arab Muslim, as is an Indian Christian from his Italian counterpart.

RJ: I wanted to have your view on the Nehruvian project of a modernized secular India. Is it still relevant? What stays of it after sixty years?

SK: Gandhi's remark about Western civilization, 'It is a good idea', also applies to the Nehruvian project. The understanding of what is secular has also changed. Secularism, as in Nehru's vision, is still relevant but not as much as it was in the 1970s. Now, it's a good idea that is not practiced much.

RJ: Do you find yourself among the modernist critics of Indian secularism, and not among the tradionalist critics?

SK: Who would be the modernist critic?

RJ: Modernists, I would say, do not condemn but criticize modern secularism for failing to find a balance between the communities, a balance between different religions. It has played too much of an authoritarian role in Indian society but without being traditionalist. The traditional view is to throw away secularism once and for all. Traditionalists believe more in reform of secularism.

SK: My view is that religion should be confined to the private sphere where every believer is completely free to practice his beliefs while the public sphere is free of all religious trappings. But I understand that what is private and what is public will remain contentious and would need a permanent, ongoing negotiation.

RJ: Would you be a critic of the French '*laicite*', which is more of a universal and republican form of secularism and which asks people, for example, not to wear the headscarf.

SK: No, I don't think so. That is going too far and has nothing to do with the law. Private means how you eat, dress, pray, and all that should not be subject to uniform laws. But marriage, divorce, inheritance, and much else which involves basic human rights belongs to the public space and should be uniformly regulated. I am thus against community-specific laws such as the Sharia for Muslims.

RJ: Because that creates a lot of problems. I remember a rape case in India which caused a huge controversy.

SK: Yes, that kind of an incident where the victim of a rape is punished, rather than the perpetrator, gives the whole community a bad name since the others get a chance to say, 'Look, how backward they are!'

RJ: The concept of harmony which you were talking about is also accompanied by more identity-giving powers, which are not always the causes of communal riots and violence. Do you see political or religious reasons for this violence?

SK: Religion, in the sense of religious belief, is certainly not a cause for violence. Tolerance of each other's religious symbols is very great in our country. If one gives people a list of Hindu–Muslim interactions, such as a Hindu eating with a Muslim (and vice versa), or a Hindu renting a house to a Muslim, and go right up to a Hindu (or Muslim) killing a Muslim (or Hindu) in a riot, then one finds that both Hindus and Muslims strongly disapprove of any actions that hurt the religious sentiments of the other community, such as the action of throwing the carcass of a cow in a temple or that of a pig in a mosque. So religion is not the cause of conflict. The problem is more anthropological than theological. For instance, the action of a Muslim girl going to the cinema with a Hindu boy attracts very strong disapproval in the Muslim community. In many parts of India, a simmering antagonism between the two communities exists, and at certain times, it can be mobilized as a threat to the identity of the community. The greatest identity threat for Muslims, not always conscious, is of the disappearance of their faith from the country as they get absorbed and overwhelmed by a host Hindu of outnumbering them. The identity threat for the Hindus is the dreaded revival of the Muslim rule.

RJ: What you are saying is that theologians do not have a problem but the masses have because they are manipulated most of the time?

SK: Yes, but they also get manipulated because there is something in them that responds and resonates to the manipulation. All the inter-faith conferences that are held after each big riot have little meaning because the theologians always agree that both the religions are peaceful and can co-exist.

RJ: So what's the way out?

SK: I wish I knew how to change mental maps, and the place that events like the Partition occupy in these maps.

Part V

Serenity Under Fire

The Mechanisms of Enemy-creating

RJ: In *Colors of Violence*, you talk about the mechanism of enemy-creating which I found very interesting, and which you say is a means of accessing the reservoir of our unwanted selves that should be kept at a psychological distance. Would you say that Muslims in India are the 'unwanted' selves of the Hindus?

SK: Very much so. This became evident to me when I was researching for *Shamans, Mystics and Doctors*. When a Hindu was possessed by a spirit, then the strongest possessing spirit was considered to be that of a Muslim who would want to eat meat and be promiscuously over-sexed. In this case, the 'Muslim' spirit represents the tempting and unwanted self of the Hindu patient.

RJ: How do you analyse Hindu suspicions of Muslim loyalty towards the Indian nation, which led to the destruction of the Babri Masjid or the killing of Muslims in Gujarat?

SK: It is the Hindu fear of the hordes of Muslim warriors who invaded medieval India that is lodged in the sub-conscious part of the Hindu mind. This fear has now transformed into images of Muslim nations coming together in an Islamic brotherhood and marching into India. Further, images of Mahmud Ghazni's annual pillaging raids, of the Mongols and the Turks destroying Hindu temples and raping Hindu women, remain embedded in the Hindu mind.

RJ: Would you say the fear of the Hindus from the Muslims (and Muslims from the Hindus) is similar to the fear from Arabs in Spain?

SK: I think the fear is also there in Spain though it is not talked about. The language of the crusades, though it is not openly used, is present in the sub-conscious.

RJ: Are there any divergences from the Indian case, say, fear of the Hindus?

SK: The divergence is that in Europe, Christians are in an overwhelming majority and feel strong, but here in India, though Hindus are in a majority, they feel weaker vis-à-vis the Muslims. When you feel weak, then the threat is seen as being much stronger than it actually is.

RJ: Could we talk about ghettos in India as we have in Europe, not just the mental ghettos but also the physical ones? Could we say that Muslims in India live in their own ghettos?

SK: Well, that is true about the Hindus also who live in the ghettos of their castes.

RJ: We can see the same kind of violence in Hindus also with regard to Muslims because of making fun of Allah or whistling at a Muslim girl. This is the reaction that comes out from the chauvinistic Muslim males. Muslims sometimes feel humiliated by the Hindus.

SK: Yes, the Muslim humiliation comes out in statements like, 'We were once the rulers here,' with an unsaid, 'See, how we have fallen from our once exalted state.' The other issue is that the Hindu represents a temptation for the Muslim which he should not succumb to. The temptation is to be free of the rigid 'thou shall' and 'thou shall not' morality of his religion. For the Muslim, a Hindu incorporates lapses from piousness, which is always a temptation. What is *haram* remains terribly attractive.

RJ: How about the demographic space? Do you think it is greatly related to violence in India?

SK: Yes, it is certainly one of the reasons for a riot. If in a town or area, the population of a community is below 25 per cent, riots won't occur since the minority community is too cowed down. Pogroms can occur, but not riots. The population of the communities has to be almost evenly matched for a riot. This is when the communities are not sure which is the stronger one and can test each other in a violent confrontation.

RJ: In your book *Colors of Violence*, you have mentioned that 'violence between different ethnic groups occur because of the struggle over the assignment of gender, a way of locating the desired role and denigrated female communities in India'. I think we have it in both the Hindu and the Muslim communities. So, once again we go back to the question of the feminine and sexuality, which no one talks about in India except a few people like you. When they talk about violence, they always think of politics, and very few go back to the idea of the sexuality and the idea of masculine–feminine. How do you see this dialectic?

SK: I see this sexualized fear more among the Hindus, the fear that they are feminine and weak in relation to the more masculine Muslims. Who is masculine and who will be 'at the top' is certainly one of the elements that goes into the making of a riot. During the anti-Sikh riots of 1984 in Delhi, many Hindus were secretly glad that the hyper-masculinity affected by the Sikhs, or rather the masculinity the Hindus ascribe to them, was being taken down a peg or two. I remember one of my patients saying, 'Serves the mother f-----s right! Always swaggering around with their cock erect. Now it is being cut off.'

RJ: It is a kind of clash of myths. When there is violence, there is also humiliation, and one of the causes of humiliation seems to exist in the hegemonizing imperatives of economic development in India, which has played a very important role.

SK: True. A loss of traditional craft identity, whether it's that of the lock-maker in Aligarh or the brass worker in Moradabad, under the hegemonizing imperatives of modernization will naturally lead to feelings of helplessness and humiliation.

RJ: There is also an additional humiliation for the traditional Indian elite, and that is the defeat of the traditional in their encounter with the West.

SK: Yes, but that is changing. I think the Muslim elite had a bigger struggle with this defeat. They retreated from the battle field and took refuge in nostalgia. I think all that is ending. Young Muslims are emerging from the weight of generations of nostalgia and withdrawal. Some nostalgia, a poisoned gift from your ancestors, will always remain but that won't stop you from going ahead and asserting yourself again in life.

The Pure and the Impure

RJ: India has become a huge tourist attraction. How has India's contact with the foreigner changed the Indian view of the foreigner? I remember that you were telling me that the owner of a cafe in Goa, who comes back in the winter season, also comes here to fulfil his sexual desires. I see that too as a way of asserting one's identity.

SK: Due to the Indian hierarchical vision, in which skin colour plays a role in determining your status, the only foreigner most Indians take seriously is the white-skinned one. Africans are looked down upon and openly scorned. Marriage to an African or any other Black will be considered as one of the worst misfortunes that can befall an Indian family. Westerners are also looked upon as being unclean at the same time as they are sucked up to. The sexual openness of the West is equated with a lack of all morality, and Western women are fair game since they are all promiscuous anyway. These contradictory attitudes create difficulty for the white foreigner too. On the one hand, he feels flattered as someone who is of a superior stock, while on the other, he gets the feeling that there is something in the Indian attitude toward him that is not quite right.

RJ: You are much by yourself when you are a blonde?

SK: Yes.

RJ: This is true anywhere in the world. Have you ever analysed this?

SK: I would imagine that it has something to do with the belief that dark is dirty while white is clean and pure. All those associations with dark and light, present in so many languages of the world—dark as being sinister, satanic, belonging to the underworld, and white as being pure, angelic—continue to live in us.

RJ: It also has to do with the sexuality part, because blondes are considered much more sexually attractive in many cultures, but dark-skinned women are not necessarily so.

SK: It is the other way round. Sexuality is strongly associated with dark skin and not only because the genitals are darker than the rest of the body. The attraction of blondes may lie in the fantasy of deflowering virginal purity.

RJ: In India, this complexion is very predominant.

SK: Yes, very much so. Complexion plays a big role in determining physical attractiveness. We are a very colour-conscious society.

RJ: But it applies only for the woman?

SK: More for the woman, yes, but it also applies to a man, though to a lesser extent. 'Dark and handsome', is not a phrase that is used here. People will say that he is dark *but* handsome or that she may be dark but is still quite good-looking. A dark hero in Bollywood movies is rare but dark villains are the rule.

RJ: What do you think is the role of colour in Hindu society, for example, why is the colour of Krishna blue and not orange?

SK: There is a whole treatise on the auspiciousness of colour. Krishna is blue as he is from a lower caste, but he is God and so one doesn't want his darkness to be a despised black. Thus he becomes blue, which is dark but is also something special.

RJ: Yes, colour plays an important role in all societies. For example, in Islam, it is green. In Turkey, the car on which the dead are put is not painted black, but green. As we are talking about Islam, I would like to talk a bit about fundamentalism and the colour of violence. I read about it in your book, *Colors of Violence*. It is interesting that you see fundamentalism as already coming, Would you say that Muslim fundamentalism in India is also a product of modernization?

SK: Yes, its location is in the elite's loss, humiliation, and nostalgia; in the masses, it is more a loss of traditional work identities. Narcissism plays an important role in a human being's life, even more than sexuality, and any scratching of our narcissistic shields invites retribution, often of a violent kind.

Suffering and Cure

RJ: You said that psychologically, fundamentalism is a theory of suffering and cure. You make a comparison with modern individualism and say that modern individualism also has to do with sufferings. What do you mean by that?

SK: Modern individualism locates the core of the individual suffering within the person—murderous rage, envy, possessive desire, and so on. Fundamentalism sees the cause of suffering outside the person—as a historical process, which is reversible. For the fundamentalist, individual and collective suffering are due to a lapse from an ideal state of religious faith, and the cure lies in restoring faith to its original pure state.

RJ: In Shiaite Islam, we have the concept of 'martyrdom', which is not there in many other religions and even in modern individualism. Also, fundamentalists view martyrdom as a way of becoming eternal. I don't think that through modern individualism, one can become timeless.

SK: No.

RJ: Do you have the same element in Hinduism?

SK: No, because martyrdom does not square well with the Hindu theory of rebirth. Since you can't become eternal, there is no point in martyrdom as you are going to be reborn anyway. Hinduism does have the concept of self-sacrifice, which is not the same as martyrdom; the motivations for the two are quite different.

RJ: We were talking about the specificity of Islam and Muslims in India. Would you say that fundamentalism in India is also of a particular kind or is it the same as everywhere else?

SK: Now it has started looking the same as elsewhere. The tide of Islamic fundamentalism outside is so strong that it seems to be washing away the specific nuances of different countries. At one time, one was proud to say that no Indian Muslim was involved in any of the international terrorist incidents but one can no longer say that. I wish it wasn't so. I wish it was possible to develop fundamentalism of our own kind, that if fundamentalism is the need of a section of Indian Muslims, then they could develop a specifically Indian fundamentalism and their own way of protest, a less violent one.

RJ: This tradition exists in India as you have a vast number of Muslims who were non-violent, like Abdul Gaffar Khan and Maulana Azad.

SK: Yes, which means that we need to be constantly reminded of them and develop that tradition.

RJ: I am sure you have concerned yourself with this like anyone else who is concerned with the problems in today's world, and somebody who is very sensitive about religion and writes about it like yourself. I am not asking for a recipe but whether you have thought of it or not. For example, I feel one way out is to engage Muslims in the process of democratization around the world, even internationally, at the level of the Middle East. Would you agree with this or do you think that there are other solutions?

SK: Certainly there are solutions, but my first step would be to find ways of reducing the violence in the interactions between the communities. You can have dislike and prejudice, but acting on them in a violent way needs to be stopped with a heavy hand, if necessary. The reduction of prejudice, bias, and tension between Hindus and Muslims will take time, but in the meanwhile, putting a stop to the violence is of fundamental importance. Here, I believe that the state's law and order machinery needs to take very strong steps to nip rising tensions between the communities in the bud, at any particular place. We know from riot situations in other countries of the world that you have a window of twenty-four hours before violence erupts, when tension starts rising, and where strong police action can stop potential violence. After that, it may be too late. Unfortunately, we have a weak state that is pulled by the interests of this or that group and almost never acts till the violence has almost run its course.

RJ: But it has to be a righteous state?

SK: Of course. I think my belief in the use of state force in stopping a riot before it even starts probably comes from my father, a magistrate.

A Fragile World

RJ: India gave birth to non-violence. Could it be used as a weapon against violence?

SK: I am doubtful of non-violence as a strategy. I am doubtful because I believe non-violence on a mass scale can only be carried out under the leadership of a charismatic personality like Gandhi, Martin Luther King, or Mandela. And these leaders are charismatic not because of their strategies or ideas but because people feel that there is something spiritual about them. People are not moved by ideas but by the person who holds them.

RJ: Friendship?

SK: It is difficult for human beings to go beyond their ego and express their love for other human beings. I think some civilizations had less trouble regarding the concept of friendship than we have today. For example, for the Greeks, the concept of friendship came alongwith with their political framework and the ethics of citizenship. Today, friendship is very difficult to find. Maybe one dimension of non-violence today is friendship.

RJ: Where do you find this concept of friendship in the Hindu view of friendship?

SK: It is one of the ways of approaching divinity. There are different ways of approaching God in Hinduism, especially in the bhakti tradition. You can approach Him as a child, or erotically as a lover, and so on. One of the ways is to regard God as *sakhi* or *sakha*, as a friend.

RJ: And also with regard to animals and nature?

SK: Yes.

RJ: India is a rare country where you have this concept of friendship with the animals?

SK: Yes, animals are a part of the divinity. All gods and goddesses have their mounts. For example, Ganesha has a rat, Shiva has a bull, Vishnu has a swan, and so on. Divinity is not singular but includes a spouse and an animal. One can say that it is a different kind of trinity: the Self, its completion by the opposite sex, and Nature.

RJ: Have animals always played a very important role in your life?

SK: I grew up in small towns where we had all sorts of animals—cows at home for milk, peacocks in the garden, chickens in the backyard, and, of course, dogs.

RJ: You still have dogs and cats as pets in your house?

SK: Yes, they are very therapeutic. First, they regulate your narcissism by demanding attention, thus forcing you to get out of your self-preoccupations, and on the other hand, they increase your self-esteem by showing how loveable you are even when you are down on yourself. Second, they teach you about love by giving it generously without being asked.

RJ: Sometimes it is easier to have animals than children and companions?

SK: I agree.

RJ: Because they are not that demanding?

SK: Yes, but also because they engage your best parts—affection and generosity, and not anger, envy, or hate as is occasionally seen among human beings.

RJ: I would like to have your view on the planet or the environment, on the dangers with which we are living today. You have not written much about it but I am interested to know what responsibility we should have towards our planet, and in general, towards the biosphere, which we are destroying because of our ego?

SK: I think here we need a change in our view of the Self, that is to think of Self as not only being based in the body and human biology, but one which is intimately connected to its surroundings, to vegetation, and animal life. That changed view would bring nature into the notion of the Self and its ideal development. Protection of the environment then becomes a part of fostering one's own intellectual, emotional, and spiritual development, and that of one's children. We should encourage research on the role of different aspects of the environment in mental development, in interpersonal sensitivity, or in empathic capability. There are many other such research projects involving the changed concept of the Self that I can easily think of. If this view of the person holds, and the kind of research I talked of starts happening, then we will have a much stronger motivation for protecting the environment. Unless you associate the protection of the environment, selfishly, with your own protection, the energy put in environmental efforts will remain low. I think the Hindu theory of rebirth hints at a similar connection. If one believes that the environment needs to be protected for one's children or, at the most, one's grandchildren, then the tendency is to say that *après moi, le deluge*. But if you believe that you yourself will come back again and again to this very world, then you will be vitally interested in the state of your present and future habitat.

RJ: It means that you can't have a future without a biosphere?

SK: Yes, and then to show how important the biosphere, in general, is to the individual, his mental development, social relationships, and so on. The emphasis has to be on its importance, not to humankind, because nobody relates generally to an abstract human kind, but to the concrete individual.

RJ: Do you believe in reincarnation?

SK: No, I sometimes wish it was a possibility, that I had this belief, but it is not so.

The Erotics of Non-Violence

RJ: Let's talks little bit about your book *Mira and the Mahatma*, where you discuss the long associations between Madeleine Slade and Gandhi through what is preserved in their autobiographies, letters, and diaries. What interested you in their relationship?

SK: When I started the novel, my interest was in discovering Gandhi as a person, to see the private face behind the public mask. This could only be done by exploring his intimate relationships rather than by looking at his political actions. But while writing the novel, Mira became more interesting as did the relationship between the two.

RJ: I saw that the title of the book in the American edition is different. It is called *The Seeker*.

SK: That is because the American publisher said that no one knows about Mira or Mahatma in the USA.

RJ: The German title is *Die Frau Die Gandhi Liebte*.

SK: *Die Frau Die Gandhi Liebte* can be read both ways, either as the woman who loved Gandhi or the woman whom Gandhi loved.

RJ: There has been a lot of speculation about Miraben's relationship with Gandhi. Did you have to go through many documents to write the story, by sifting between the fiction and the reality?

SK: There is a lot of material available in the form of letters written by them to each other, Miraben's autobiography, and other people's reminiscences. So there was no dearth of material. From all accounts, it was a very passionate relationship.

RJ: That is one of the reasons why you didn't choose Kasturba's character?

SK: There is also a sub-text of 'East meets West' in the novel, which would have been absent in Kasturba.

RJ: Of course, she is a very particular person. She is very solitary in the beginning. She has relations with plants and animals more than with human beings and suddenly she gets mesmerized by the personality of Gandhi. Some people say that she fainted the first time she saw Gandhi. In one of her letters to Romain Rolland, she writes that 'whenever she touches Gandhi she feels the eternal'.

SK: She was always mystically and spiritually inclined, and Gandhi for her was the Spirit incarnate. She *was* really 'The Seeker'. She was looking for a container for all her longings and yearnings, spiritual and sexual, and these longings got focused on Gandhi.

RJ: This is the essence of all your psychological work in the domain of historical figures. As you say, if a person is seeking something then he/she will go and find it in somebody. Like many of the followers of Sai Baba or Shri Mataji are doing today. Were you criticized by some of the followers of Gandhi because of this work?

SK: Yes, in the beginning when they had not read the book, they were only reacting to the title which they found provocative. They thought that it was some scandalous story. There were incidents of burning of the book in Delhi and Ahmedabad the day after its publication by some self-styled Gandhians. There was a small procession in Delhi with a donkey in front with a placard and my name written on it hung around its neck. The placard, referring to a line in one of Gandhi's favourite *bhajans*, read '*Kakar ko sanmati de bhagwan*'—'God give Kakar good sense'. I thought it was all very funny. In a TV discussion, people like Nirmala Deshpande were furious but when I asked them, 'Have you read the book', they all said 'no'. Her whole point was how I dared write about her icon as a flesh and blood man. He is so high and you are so low, she said, and how can an ant look at the sky and things like that. They were very upset but it soon subsided as there was nothing in the book that would lower Gandhi in any sane person's eyes. In fact, Gandhi has revealed much more shocking things about himself.

RJ: It shows the gap between Gandhians and Gandhi himself?

SK: Yes, a huge gap. Most Gandhians sorely lack the humour Gandhi had.

RJ: Gandhi would have approved of your book more because he denied calling himself Gandhi. People try to make a cult of Gandhi but Gandhi himself was against any cult?

SK: Yes. In fact, the book is quite admiring of Gandhi but it makes him human.

RJ: In several of her imaginary letters to Rolland, Mira talks about her love for Gandhi. She said that it opens her like a flower and heightens her sense of herself and the world around her. Do you find anything erotic in Mira's love for Gandhi or is it pure 'agape'?

SK: I don't think it was purely agape. There is an erotic dimension to it. Agape means selfless love. The old word for 'self' is 'soul', and I doubt whether anyone would want soulless love. Agape is neither worth receiving nor worth giving if it is without eros. Real agape must be infused with the passion of the eros.

RJ: Like earlier Christianity that talks about an erotic part to it?

SK: Yes.

RJ: There are two perceptions of Gandhi. One is the Western one, which sometimes goes to the extremes, and situates him in historical times. The other is the Indian one, that situates him in mythical times, which is very dangerous as it goes far from Gandhi.

SK: Yes, I think you are quite right.

RJ: How can one understand a charismatic personality like Gandhi or any other personality of the twenty-first century by writing about him?

SK: I think that if you raise a person high up into the firmament, then you can only worship him. But if you identify with a person and feel close to him, then the person's ideas and thoughts also affect you much more than if you merely worshipped him. I feel nearer to Gandhi and his ideas after discovering our shared humanity than I ever did before, when he was just an icon.

Towards a Spiritual Century

RJ: How do you perceive the dialectic between the relative and the absolute in our century?

SK: I think there are people like me who try to find a balance between the two as they do between the historical and the mythical.

RJ: Lewis Mumford says that every transformation of man, except perhaps that which produced the Neolithic culture, has rested on a new metaphysical or ideological base. What would you say is a new metaphysical base of the global civilization that is emerging today?

SK: I am not sure where it is going but I would call it the resurgence of the romantic imagination. Romantic not in the pejorative sense but the romantic imagination of people like Einstein in science, Kant in philosophy, and so on. And Gandhi would be the central figure of romantic imagination in political and social action. Altruism is a part of this romantic resurgence as is an increase in our empathy. We human beings are a selfish lot but are also capable of empathy and altruistic behaviour. The metaphysical base of the emerging global civilization for me is an empathy for all kinds of beings, including animals, and for nature. The base is an extended notion of the self that is not limited to your body and your mind but includes others, where one increasingly sees one's self in others.

RJ: So, with a dialogical philosophy, we can go beyond the ontology of the subject?

SK: And beyond the objectness of others.

RJ: A key element of hope in the new age agenda is the information revolution, which has created myriad networks, and which gives us a grand vision of the planetary transformation. I think that also increases togetherness and connectedness.

SK: Yes, all that helps in increasing empathy. People watch pictures of suffering children, ravages suffered by victims of war on television, and feel a stab of empathy for them even though they may be separated by continents.

RJ: But don't you think there is the possibility of a misuse of information technology that we have—the internet or satellite communications. There is also a danger of manipulation.

SK: Certainly, but that is part of all technology and there is no denying the power of human selfishness.

RJ: So we need a critical reflection on it.

SK: Yes. Constantly.

RJ: In the secularized West, for a long time, psychology replaced religion as a centre of human concern. But it seems that people are looking more and more at religion and spirituality to find answers to their modern anxieties. How do you as a psychoanalyst see this trend of going back to religion, spirituality, and culture?

SK: I think this too is part of the romantic resurgence. I would look at it positively. People want more than the common human condition promised by psychology. They want to rise to a higher, or at least a different, level of consciousness. Psychology is also going in two directions: one is completely biological wherein the brain is the basis of mind and consciousness, and the second is more transpersonal wherein the brain is the receiver for signals that come from outside the person.

RJ: When you talk about revolution, one part of it is empathy, being attentive to others and the nation. Don't you think there is a negative side to it, especially religious fundamentalism?

SK: Yes.

RJ: They go together?

SK: Yes, that too, is unavoidable. The dark side is always there and this has been the valuable contribution of depth psychology, both Freudian and Jungian, to always remind us of the existence of the shadow.

RJ: We have an explosion of literature on the scientific evidences of riots. Do you agree with this scientific inclination towards religion or spirituality?

SK: I think that the base of spirituality is not science and that it doesn't need scientific approbation. Not that I am not interested in the scientific approach, say to psychology. I remain a Freudian with his hermeneutics of suspicion and that is best served by science. But I am also a romantic with its hermeneutics of idealization, which does not need science but looks toward inspiration and values imagination as much, or even more, than reason.

RJ: How about someone like the Dalai Lama talking about science?

SK: I think he is a little too impressed by science. It is fine for those who need scientific proofs; I don't think they are necessary.

RJ: How do you explain the rise of interest in Buddhism?

SK: There are two reasons for this. The first is that Buddhism is, in a sense a secular religion—Buddha's silence when asked about the existence of God—so you can be both religious and secular if you are a modern Buddhist. The second is Buddhism's claim to be scientific as it believes in questioning every assumption and rejecting even the most cherished one if the evidence is to the contrary. I am organizing a seminar by a German foundation next year on 'Spirituality and Depth Psychology', and four of the eight papers are about Buddhism. Jungian and Freudian analysts who are interested in spirituality have their first entry to this realm through Buddhism. In a sense, Buddhism is an export version of Hinduism wherein all the messy stuff has been taken out.

RJ: The kind of Buddhism which is lived in the West is at times popularized and vulgarized because most of the people who practise it do not know about the Buddhist school of thought and philosophy, or about the debate which has been going on inside the school.

SK: They look at it as a collection of spiritually informed and useful mental health techniques.

RJ: Because of the reactions that you get from the common people you assume that there are no fundamentalists in Buddhism, but people like the Dalai Lama have said that this is not true. I think the image which people have of Buddhism is a false one.

SK: Yes, part of the image is certainly false and Buddhism has such an attractive pin-up man in the Dalai Lama.

A Peaceful Eye

RJ: You have turned seventy this year. So when you look back at your academic work, how do you relate to it?

SK: I am fortunate to have lived all my life in a peaceful world where I and my loved ones were never affected by the horrors of war and violence. I was lucky that I had no constraints on my thought or the freedom of their expression. I was lucky to have had so many choices and that I almost always selected the most exciting option.

RJ: If you were to have a second life, would you like to be a psychologist again?

SK: No. I don't think so. I have already done it and would like to move on. If I had the talent, or rather that kind of a genius (talent is fine for most fields but not for poetry), I would like to be a poet but a poet with an inherited wealth and not a poor one.

RJ: Do you have preference for any particular kind of poetry in Indian culture and also in Western culture?

SK: Yes, Yeats, Rilke, Neruda, and Rothke are my favourite Western poets; Ghalib and Faiz my favourite Urdu poets.

RJ: Most of the Sufi and mystic poetry?

SK: Oh, yes.

RJ: Amir Khusro?

SK: No, too difficult.

RJ: Blake, maybe?

SK: He is too well-known. It doesn't surprise you when you read him.

RJ: You like to be surprised?

SK: I like to be surprised, even astonished. Good poetry can keep on surprising you, but Blake is so familiar that he doesn't surprise any more. And as someone said, God is surprise.

RJ: Now about music. Would you have liked to be a musician?

SK: Yes, but...

RJ: After having a life with so many ups and downs, you are now living in Goa away from the turmoil. Do you find yourself happy in this environment?

SK: Yes, I am very content. Happiness is transitory by its very nature; it is not what you strive for but what comes to you unexpectedly as a gift. I am more content in my autumn, or should I say winter, than I was in my spring, in spite of youth's many happy, even ecstatic moments. Sometimes, I wish I had been less lazy and less inclined towards the pleasures of sensuality when I was younger. But these are idle imaginings, not serious disaffections. Schopenhauer once said that at the end of his life, no man, if he be sincere and in possession of his faculties, would ever wish to go through it again. Looking back sincerely, and I hope in possession of my faculties, I would still live the same life all over again. But I hope I am not tempting the gods by saying this, since there is perhaps still some life left in me.